Be Free

John Alan Shope

Copyright © 2018 John Alan Shope

All rights reserved.

"Just as we can know the ocean because it always tastes of salt, we can recognize enlightenment, because it always tastes of freedom." Gautama Buddha

"The secret to happiness is freedom…and the secret to freedom is courage." Thucydides

"You will know the truth and the truth will set you free." Jesus of Nazareth

"He has sent me to proclaim freedom to the captives and recovering of sight to the blind, to set free those who are oppressed." Jesus of Nazareth

"The only way to deal with an unfree world is to become so absolutely free that your very existence is an act of rebellion." Albert Camus

"Letting go gives us freedom, and freedom is the only condition for happiness." Thich Nhat Hanh

"For freedom, Christ has set us free. Stand firm, therefore, and do not submit again to a yoke of slavery." Paul of Tarsus

"Educate and inform the whole mass of the people. They are the only sure reliance for the preservation of our freedom." Thomas Jefferson

"The secret of freedom lies in educating people, whereas the secret of tyranny is in keeping them ignorant." Maximilien Robespierre

"Most people do not really want freedom because freedom assumes responsibility, and most people do not want that responsibility." Sigmund Freud

"The truth will set you free, but first it will piss you off." Joe Klaas

"Those who deny freedom to others, deserve it not for themselves." Abraham Lincoln

"Better to die fighting for freedom then be a prisoner all the days of your life." Bob Marley

"Freedom lies in being bold." Robert Frost

"For to be free is not merely to cast off one's chains, but to live in a way that respects and enhances the freedom of others." Nelson Mandela

"Once a man has tasted freedom, he will never be content to be a slave." Walt Disney

"Truth is like the sun. You can shut it out for a time, but it ain't going away." Elvis Presley

This book is dedicated to Siddhārtha Gautama (Buddha), Yeshua bar Yosef (Jesus), Giovanni di Pietro di Bernardone (St. Francis) and all those who have dared to be free from religious, political and economic exploitation, regardless of the cost.

johnalanshope@gmail.com

Contents

Introduction 9
Freedom from Religious Exploitation 13
   My Story 13
   Religion Affects Us All 18
   Difficulty of Letting Go 21
   Religious Division 25
   Religious Dishonesty 28
   The Bible 31
   Sin 45
   Jesus 53
      The Evolution of Jesus 54
      The True Jesus of History 60
      The Resurrection of Jesus 62
      Jesus and Buddha 68
      Setting Jesus Free from Christianity 76
Freedom from Political & Economic Exploitation 85
   Two Economic Worldviews 87
   Lessons from the Past 89
   "Liberal" 92
   Victim's Top 6 List 96
   People Become Like Their God 100

- Freedom from Addiction 107
  - The Nature of Addiction 108
  - Breaking Free 110
  - Top 5 Addictions 114
- Freedom from Fear 123
  - Painful Childhood Events 123
  - Fear of Death 127
    - The Gift of Life 129
    - A Larger Sense of Self 135
    - Consciousness – the Final Frontier 141
    - Evidence for One Universal Consciousness 145
    - Who Are You? 154
    - Individuality 159
    - Why Are We Here? 165
    - Somewhere Over the Rainbow 168
- Freedom to Enjoy Life Responsibly 175
  - Oneness 178
  - Pain and Suffering 182
- Epilogue 187
  - 5 Stages of Freedom 187
- Appendix 193

Introduction

At some point, we all ask big questions - sometimes after the death of a loved one, sometimes after being confronted with our own impending death. Not everyone asks, but most do, sooner or later.

The questions go like this. What's life all about? Why am I here? Does life have meaning and purpose or is it just a series of random events? Is there life after death or is this all there is? What should my priorities be? What should I pass on to my children? Are there any absolutes to guide me through life or is everything relative? If there are answers, where can I find them?

Some seek answers in religion or mystical experiences. They turn to Bibles, preachers, churches, temples, synagogues or mosques. Others turn to philosophy or science, refusing to be chained to the past, regardless of how sacred the traditions. Some turn to art or music, believing that ultimate truth cannot be expressed in words alone. Still, others become activists, believing that what you do is more meaningful than what you say, think or believe.

Some have decided there are no answers, at least none we humans can grasp right now. Their focus is simply on making a living, enjoying life and spending time with loved ones. Like most of us, they are driven by survival, sex and the pleasure that comes from making sacrifices for those they love. They're not asking the "big questions" – at least not right now.

Are there answers? Absolutely, but they're more complicated than most expect. The best answers usually raise more questions. Truth is always a work in progress and full of surprises. It requires that we be brutally honest and dare to think for ourselves.

The first section of this book is written especially for "Bible believing" evangelicals and others who have deep religious roots. 60% of American adults consider themselves religious. That's down from 73% in 2005, but still a significant number.

Far too many, just like me, have been brainwashed as children and young adults. I took a class in seminary that focused on religious cults. As my professor was describing the characteristics of a cult, I remember thinking that my own Baptist faith met all the criteria. It was the elephant in the room that none of us were bold enough to acknowledge at the time.

Yes, tens of millions of Americans have been brainwashed by a pervasive religious culture, and we need to be set free – not just for our sake but for the sake of our children and our world. But letting go of long held beliefs can be difficult and painful. This book will help you do that.

The rest of the book deals with issues beyond religion that affect us all. All of us are exploited by politics. We need to step back and see the bigger picture that politicians don't want us to see. History can help us do that.

All of us are exploited to various degrees by our own addictions. Addiction is not just about drugs. Understanding the dynamics of addiction will help all of us live more freely.

All of us fear death at some level - both our own and the death of those we love. Religion and politics exploit that fear. There are better and more credible ways to confront the anxiety that death causes and even find hope. The last section of this book will explore this in depth.

We need freedom. We need to wake up. We need courage to leave the herd, think outside the box and color outside the lines. Knowledge is power, and truth will set you free - although both will make you uncomfortable at first. Nevertheless, keep reading and join me in a bold and honest search for truth, freedom and happiness.

John Alan Shope

Freedom from Religious Exploitation

"Religion is regarded by the common people as true, by the wise as false, and by the rulers as useful," Seneca, Roman philosopher.

My Story

I was fairly religious as a child. I grew up in the "Bible Belt". True to my Baptist roots, I went through the ritual they refer to as "being saved" at the age of 12. Like many, I drifted away from the church during high school and college, but after a somewhat traumatic personal experience, I (as the Baptists would say) "re-dedicated my life to Christ" while in college.

I earned a Bachelor's degree from Hannibal LaGrange College and then a Masters degree from Southwestern Baptist Theological Seminary, pastoring churches in Missouri and Texas along the way.

I attended Southwestern Seminary before the conservatives took over in the mid 90s. At the time, Southwestern was the largest Protestant seminary in the world. Before this rather hostile takeover, students were encouraged to think freely and ask hard questions - which I did.

As a pastor, I continued to ask hard questions, and I struggled with much of what I saw behind the scenes. The theological inconsistencies, the judgmental attitudes, the institutional politics and the hypocrisy of people in general became problematic, to say the least. I soon became a pastor with more questions than answers.

One of the first things I questioned was why most of the church's money stayed inside the church to maintain the institution, rather than going outside the church to help the poor. Spending most of our money on institutional maintenance, as most churches do, seemed very inconsistent with the teachings of Jesus.

A wise old minister made an astute observation years ago. He quoted one of the first disciples of Jesus who said to a poor cripple man, "Silver and gold have I none, but what I do have I give you. In the name of Jesus, stand up and walk."

The minister went on to remark that, today, the church can no longer say to a cripple man, "stand up and walk," but it does have plenty of silver and gold. Unfortunately, most of that "silver and gold" stays in the church, and that became an issue for me.

If we know anything at all about Jesus and his first followers, we know that sharing one's possessions with the poor was a major priority. According to the Bible, Jesus instructed his first followers to sell all their possessions and give the money to the poor. They actually tried something like that in the first years following his death. Obviously, most modern churches have conveniently overlooked this major part of Jesus' teachings – but I couldn't.

Not only did I question the church's relationship with money, I also questioned the whole idea of creating a place where people could come together for a couple of hours on Sunday morning to feel good. Don't misunderstand. There's nothing wrong with that, and a lot of people need that. The problem is, there's nothing about that in the teachings of Jesus. Yet, for most Christians, that is the primary way they follow Jesus – they "go to church".

It gradually became clear to me that my main job was to coordinate, orchestrate and facilitate this Sunday morning gathering. People expected a pleasant atmosphere, good music, an interesting sermon and childcare.

Instead of helping people become more like Jesus, I ended up being a marketeer, a fundraiser and an entertainer. Again, there's nothing wrong with any of that, as long as you call it what it is and don't equate it with following Jesus.

Obviously, as a minister, I did other things which were important. Occasionally, I was able to help people financially using a small fund set aside for that purpose. I did a lot of counseling. I conducted funerals and weddings. I tried to be there for my parishioners during times of crisis.

Thankfully, seminary gave me the basic skills I needed to help people in need; but that role was always overshadowed by administrative duties and the need to increase attendance on Sunday morning.

I finally conceded that this whole enterprise we call "church" had little to do with the primary teachings of Jesus, who obviously never envisioned the scenario that plays out in most churches every Sunday morning.

Because of this and numerous other inconsistencies, I knew I could no longer make my living as a Baptist minister. I no longer believed what I was being paid to promote and defend. It wasn't necessarily a bad thing; it just wasn't what it claimed to be.

Feeling extremely frustrated - even exploited in some ways by the institution - and after a lot of painful soul searching, I finally decided to resign from the church. It was a risky move, but the only path I could follow in good conscience. My family and I were more fortunate than many who take similar risks in that I soon found another way to make a living.

During my years as a pastor, it had become absolutely clear to me that "God" was far bigger than my conservative, evangelical theology. After leaving my Baptist roots, I started exploring more liberal branches of Christianity. The differences were refreshing and even healing to some degree; but even in those larger, more inclusive tents, "God" was still too small.

I continued to serve other churches in various ways, met many intriguing people and made wonderful new friends. Still, I kept finding myself disenchanted with institutional Christianity. I kept finding as much, if not more, honesty and truth outside the church than inside.

But it was hard to let go of something I had given so much of my life to. It was hard to leave things that were familiar and safe. And, what if I was wrong? I had been assured by more than one that I was "going to hell" for forsaking my evangelical roots.

For me, much of the difficulty was separating Jesus from the religion that bears his name. I had spent so much of my life studying, trusting, following and believing in Jesus. It may sound silly to those outside the church, but I had fallen in love with Jesus. There was no doubt in my mind, and I am still convinced, that his teachings changed my life for the better.

But who was Jesus? I'll discuss this in more detail later, but I finally realized that being a Christian and going to church was not the same thing as following Jesus. Ultimately, I was able to let go of the church's Jesus. I discovered a far more authentic Jesus outside the church. With Martin Luther King, I could finally declare, "Free at last, free at last - thank God almighty I'm free at last."

The Jesus outside the church was not threatened by science, history, other religions, psychology or philosophy. The Jesus outside the church was far less judgmental than the church's Jesus. The Jesus outside the church was free from the selfish and exploitive fear mongering that dominated the church's Jesus.

Conservative Muslims, Jews and Buddhists would do well to re-examine traditional versions of their respective founders. Religion always betrays its founders and makes them less free.

Mohammed, Abraham, Moses, Buddha and Jesus were all about setting people free from religion, not creating new ones. They were a threat to the religions and the politicians of their day. Why do subsequent generations keep returning to the religious and political slavery their forefathers left behind?

In the years that followed, I continued exploring philosophy, psychology and various branches of science. I began to meditate regularly and pursue a simpler lifestyle. I gradually broke free from the religious brainwashing that had dominated my life for so long.

Ultimately, I reached a place where divisions between secular and sacred, religious and non-religious, spiritual and natural no longer made sense. I started seeing everything as "sacred". I realized that everything and everyone deserve honor and respect. Everyone and everything belongs.

Unfortunately, humans are still starting churches and building temples - still judging and dividing. "God is here, but not there". "God is with us, but not with them". I'm reminded of a verse in the Bible, "the Most High doesn't live in temples made by human hands. Heaven is God's throne, and the earth is God's footstool."

As an ancient Taoist wrote, "The God that can be named is not God." Whatever mystery the name "God" tries to point to - that mystery is far bigger than all our churches, temples and religions. But people keep starting, building and promoting churches and temples, especially in America.

For me and millions of others, religion may have had some value - I'm not sure. I think the bad in religion always outweighs the good. John Lennon was probably right to imagine "no religion, too." Either way, there comes a time when we need to move on.

People still ask me today, "Where do you go to church?" I often smile and say, "I graduated." There comes a time when we need to wake up, break free and move on from the division, the hypocrisy and the exploitation that religion so often embodies.

Religion Affects Us All

Even those of us who do not consider ourselves religious are still exploited by religion in subtle and indirect ways. I know many, especially in the Bible Belt (Southern and Midwestern United States), who never go to church, nor do they practice Christianity in any meaningful way; yet they are very quick to defend basic Christian ideas related to Jesus, hell, or some other belief passed on from their parents or grandparents.

Perhaps this sort of minimal faith gives them some degree of comfort, but it also makes them vulnerable to politicians who exploit them with vague religious language and divisive propaganda. They then help elect those same politicians who, in turn, affect all of us.

The influence of religion on modern American politics is shocking. As I write these words, more and more politicians with questionable moral character are being supported by Christians. The church seems to have adapted an "end justifies the means" mentality that would not have been acceptable a few decades ago. Money and power now seem to "trump" (no pun intended) ethics and honesty.

Consider how conservative Christians have managed to potentially affect our nation's foreign policy in ways that would have been unheard of just a few decades ago. As conservative politicians become more dependent on the conservative Christian vote, decisions regarding Israel and the Middle East are being made, at least partly, to please that part of the political base.

The evangelical belief that Jesus will return to earth physically after certain things happen in Israel, is motivating some politicians, including our current President (Donald Trump), to make decisions in harmony with those irrational and dangerous beliefs.

The frightening truth that many Americans seem to miss is how prevalent these bazaar "end time" beliefs are among modern Christians. A recent series of books about the Rapture and 2nd Coming of Jesus – the Left Behind series – sold 60,000,000 copies. That suggests a readership of over 100 million Americans. A recent major movie was based on these books.

The world view presented in these books is a modern invention that was never part of historical Christianity. But worse, it creates a worldview based on ancient apocalyptic myths that completely distort Middle East history and the state of our modern world. It encourages irresponsible foreign policy decisions that threaten global security. I hope there are enough rational conservatives to ultimately challenge this very real threat to America and the world.

As an interesting side note, the book of Revelation (the last book in the Bible) upon which these "end time" novels and movies are based, rather than describing some future apocalyptic "second coming of Christ" at the end of the world, actually describes what happened to the Jesus movement during its infancy 1800 years ago. The book of Revelation describes a world ruler (Anti-Christ or Beast) who joins forces with a powerful religious leader (False Prophet) to rule the world and persecute those who challenge their power.

This is exactly what happened in the early fourth century when the Roman Emperor Constantine joined forces with the Bishop of Rome to establish Christianity as the official religion of the Roman Empire. The Roman Emperor and the Roman Bishop were the anti-Christ and the False Prophet described metaphorically in the book of Revelation.

Among the numerous groups who were persecuted were those sincere followers of Jesus who realized what was happening and refused to be part of the new system. Many fled to the desert and other isolated areas, giving birth to what later became the ascetic and monastic branches of Christianity.

The Christian church continued playing the same role for the next 150 years. Then, after the fall of the Roman Empire, it continued to maintain power across Europe by joining forces with other political rulers and forming what historians call the Holy Roman Empire.

The Christian religion continues this pattern of exploitation today. The rise of the religious right during the past 50 years in America serves as another example of the dangerous and destructive collusion that so often takes place between religion and politics.

Some conservative Christian groups have long recognized what I just described, but mistakenly limit it to the Roman Catholic Church. What such hypocrisy fails to see is that every branch of Christianity - Protestant, Evangelical, Orthodox and Roman Catholic - is part of that exploitive process that began 1800 years ago. Overall, the Christian religion and the Christian church are still as "anti-Christ" and "anti-Jesus" as they were from the start.

Almost every time religious and political forces join together, the bad things described metaphorically in the book of Revelation take place in some form or fashion. And it seems that the more conservative the forces are, the more dangerous they are. Unfortunately, not just religious people, but all of society is ultimately affected.

Beyond foreign policy concerns, modern American Christianity also poses a threat to U.S. domestic policy. Millions of Christians support politicians who continue to weaken social safety nets that are so vital to the poor and aged, as well as take unjust positions related to criminal justice and prisons. These are not positions Jesus would support by any stretch of the imagination; yet, the vast majority of conservative Christians (over 75% at the time of this writing) continue to support these policies.

How is it that politicians and other political forces continue to use Christianity and the institutional Christian church so effectively for their own selfish ends? Basically, it comes down to three things. Many conservative politicians are skilled at using vague Christian terminology, which obviously appeals to millions of Christians. Second, affluent Christians and affluent politicians both have similar economic views, which, in spite of Jesus' warnings, allow money to be a driving force. Third, conservative politicians are masters at exploiting complicated and divisive moral issues such as abortion.

Abortion is a complicated issue and no politician, Republican or Democrat, is "pro-abortion" in the way conservative Christians and conservative politicians often claim. Sometimes, a pregnant woman must choose between the lesser of two evils. The issues are not black and white and a strict law restricting all abortions does not take into account the complexities that sometimes arise.

Abortion should not be taken lightly or seen as simply another method of birth control. But to label those who simply want to acknowledge the complexity of the issue and include the mother in the decision as "pro-abortion" or "baby killers" is disingenuous and dishonest.

Still, that simplistic and extreme approach appeals to evangelicals who end up affecting the rest of us by electing politicians who conveniently exploit that issue.

Difficulty of Letting Go

"The cave you fear to enter holds the treasure you seek," Joseph Campbell

Throughout this book, I will use words and phrases like "journey", "change" and "letting go". I do so because this is the nature of life. Your life is a journey. A major problem with religion is that it sabotages that journey. To keep moving forward, you have to be willing to change and let go of the past. Religion doesn't like that, because most religions are heavily invested in the past.

It's hard to grow up, leave home and move to a new place. Change is uncomfortable. Religion exploits that natural resistance to change. But to remain free and happy, you must keep moving forward, which means you must learn to let go.

I spent most my adult life studying the Bible, and I still quote it often. In spite of how the church dishonors, distorts and devalues it, the Bible contains a lot of insightful and inspiring stories. People would do well to stop listening to preachers exploit it, and occasionally just read it for themselves, especially the teachings of Jesus. They will find that it says a lot about letting go of the past.

For example, Mary Magdalene was one of Jesus' closest disciples. His death was difficult for her. She obviously did not want to let go of something that had brought her so much healing and joy. According to the Christian New Testament, she was the first person to experience the presence of Jesus after his death. Interestingly, Jesus first words to her in the Bible were, "Do not cling to me" (John 20:17). In other words, she must let go of her old ideas about Jesus and start seeing him in a new way.

In another Biblical story, Peter was arguing with Jesus because Jesus was not the kind of "messiah" Peter expected. According to Matthew, Jesus said to Peter, "Get behind Me, Satan! You are a stumbling block to me; for you are not setting your mind on God's interests, but man's" (Matthew 16:23). Like Mary Magdalene, Peter had to let go of his old ideas about Jesus.

In order to experience the freedom Jesus offered his first followers, they had to question and finally let go of the traditional religious culture they were raised in. It was hard and they even had to deal with Jesus' early and untimely death. But, through his example and teachings, they finally broke free from the religious and political prisons they were in.

Saint Paul, who never actually met the historical Jesus, wrote half the New Testament, and most historians consider him, rather than Jesus, to be the founder of Christianity. This, by the way, may be part of the sentiment behind a billboard I once saw depicting a picture of Jesus saying, "Don't blame me for Christianity."

Regardless, Paul, who was one of the most respected Jewish leaders of his day, wrote how his earlier Jewish religion served as a vehicle that ultimately led him to the freedom he found in the teachings of Jesus. But he had to ultimately leave Judaism behind in order to embrace that freedom.

Interestingly, if you read the letters of Paul in chronological order, rather than the order in which they are found in the Bible, you will clearly see that Paul himself kept evolving theologically and spiritually. The Paul who wrote 1 Thessalonians is very different from the Paul who wrote Romans. Continuing his spiritual evolution, the Paul who wrote Romans is very different from the Paul who wrote Ephesians.

Not surprisingly, when you finally get to 1 and 2 Timothy, you see a very institutional Paul, who was probably not Paul at all, but a leader of the now institutionalized church, trying to exploit Paul's name and reputation.

Due to their unhealthy and irrational approach to scripture, Evangelical churches refuse to acknowledge this evolution in Paul and his writings; but it's an obvious occurrence in his journey toward freedom.

In order to be free, you and I must also let ourselves evolve and let go of long held beliefs. If these beliefs have been drilled into us over and over again since childhood, it's hard. In fact, somewhat like the act of forgiveness, it usually takes awhile, and will probably include periods of doubt and relapse.

As described above, my own process of leaving Christianity took many years. In fact, I left several times but kept falling back into a different version, thinking this version may be different. After my Baptist years, I spent years as an Episcopalian, then an Anglican. Next, my wife and I became Catholic for several years. In between these major involvements, I also explored Pentecostal Christianity as well as several non-denominational churches.

It's hard to let go of such a major part of who you are. It's hard to finally leave behind a part of your life that included so many good friends and valuable experiences. But I finally had to accept that the bad outweighed the good, and that there were much healthier ways to find truth and happiness.

Religion was part of my journey, and I wouldn't change much of it, because my wife and children were also part of that journey. But it was never meant to be the end of my journey.

Buddha described early religious experience as being like a boat that takes us from one shore to the next. But once we've arrived on the new shore, the boat is no longer useful. We leave the boat behind and take a different mode of travel across the land. It's the same with our journey through life.

Freedom requires that you boldly continue your journey. Beware of those who try to keep you enslaved. Don't be a pawn in their game.

Don't continue to feed their egos and sacrifice yourself to their gods and their agendas. Declare your independence.

During the 15th century protestant reformation, while thousands were rebelling against the exploitive dogmas of the Roman Catholic church, Martin Luther wrote to his fellow insurgents, "Love God and sin boldly." We all need that kind of courage.

When we humans are at our best, there should be something inside us that admires the classic tale of the Starship Enterprise, whose mission was "to explore strange new worlds, to seek out new life and new civilizations, to boldly go where no one has gone before."[1]

The same Bible that so many religious leaders selfishly use to exploit and manipulate the masses has also been used time and time again throughout history to inspire revolutions and declarations of independence. I could list page after page of verses from the Bible that inspire such freedom. Here's just one from the book of Isaiah. "Forget the former things; do not dwell on the past. See, I am doing a new thing!" (Isaiah 43:18). God, or whatever you want to call ultimate reality, is always doing a new thing.

Finally, although I seriously doubt if the church's version of Jesus comes anywhere close to the real Jesus, here are words attributed to him in the Bible that probably do capture a crucial part of who he was. While in the synagogue, reading from the book of Isaiah, Jesus boldly declared, "He (God) has sent me to proclaim freedom to the captives and recovering of sight to the blind, to set free those who are oppressed" (Luke 4:18, Isaiah 61:1).

As one who no longer identifies as a Christian, but still tries to follow the teachings of Jesus, I encourage you to let the teachings of Jesus set you free, rather than keep you captive to exploitive religious institutions and outdated worldviews.

---

[1] Spoken by William Shatner at the beginning of each episode of Star Trek, a science fiction TV series debuting in 1966.

Religious Division

Like almost all religion, Christianity is both divisive and dishonest. Consider how divisive it is. Most of the time, it is our emotions, not our intellect, that determines our choices and our beliefs. We believe what we want to believe. The smarter we are, the easier it is to justify our beliefs, even though those justifications would not stand up to careful scrutiny. We humans are very good at promoting facts that support our current beliefs while ignoring facts that challenge our current beliefs.

As I write this book, cable news outlets such as Fox, CNN and MSNBC have taken advantage of this to maintain their ratings. Fox tends to ignore facts that challenge conservative beliefs, while CNN and MSNBC occasionally ignore facts that challenge liberal beliefs. All three will give representatives from the "other side" a voice, but it's seldom a strong voice; nor will they give opposing voices nearly as much time as voices that support the views of their audience. All three "preach to the choir". Unfortunately, this approach to journalism keeps us from seeing all sides of important issues.

For what it's worth, several analyses suggest that Fox news is more one sided than the other two, and that CNN is the most balanced; but, once again, a conservative audience will easily find reasons to reject such a negative critique of their favorite news source.

Religion divides us in the same way. It creates an "us" and "them" mentality. God has chosen "us" and rejected "them". We possess the truth, they don't. There's little compromise and very few gray areas. It's mostly black and white - all or nothing. The choices seem to always be "either/or" rather than "both/and". Conservative religion, especially, is horribly divisive because of its unwillingness to evolve and consider alternative views.

Christianity has always been divisive. Over the course of Christian history, there were many controversial issues. Once "the powers that be" (Bishops, Popes, Emperors, Kings, Councils) decided which side was "right", those on the other side were labeled "heretics" and often put to death.

In addition to the early debates regarding who Jesus was, the church also debated what books should be included in the Bible, how the Bible was to be interpreted, the meaning of the cross, the nature of the true church, the meaning of the Lord's Supper, the role of priests, and so on. The debates led to anger, intolerance and even war. Unsurprisingly, the theological issues were often more political than spiritual.

Unfortunately, Christianity is still just as divisive. Today, we have almost 30,000 Christian denominations – no wonder the average American is so confused regarding what Christians actually believe. And, as always, the division spills over into our politics, our culture and the very fabric of our society.

Sometimes it feels like we are still fighting the Civil War, which supposedly ended over 150 years ago. We seem to be struggling with the same racial, economic and cultural issues we struggled with then. Conservatives, especially in the rural South and Midwest, seem to want to hold on to a past that other Americans want to move away from. They seem to want to return to an era characterized by bigotry, blindness and fear-mongering; which was fueled to a large degree by religion.

I say this in love, but there is a heaviness that many can feel in parts of our country where religion plays a dominate role. I feel it when I travel around the United States. I talk to others who notice the same phenomenon. They use words like "depression", "darkness", "fearfulness", "anxiety" and "anger".

It seems that many conservative religious people are convinced they are fighting a war against other Americans. Their feelings are so strong that their towns literally feel like war zones. When I travel to less religious areas, there seems to be more lightness and freedom. People seem to smile more and exhibit less stress. Those who allow religion to isolate them from the rest of society seem to be paying a price, both physically and mentally.

Be Free

Tolerance and Civil Dialogue

To unify our society, we must all be willing to live and let live without judging and excluding. We must be willing to engage in honest and humble dialogue without getting defensive and angry. As long as people from other cultures, religions and lifestyles are looked down on or seen as a threat, true community is impossible.

In the Biblical book of Acts, the mature and respected Jewish leader Gamaliel gave wise counsel to those Jews who wanted to label the first Christians as "heretics". He said, in essence, "Be patient. Listen and learn. If this new movement is from God, you won't be able to stop it. If it's not from God, it will slowly die on its own without your help." Unfortunately, while his advice was followed initially, It was ultimately ignored, causing Christians and Jews to become bitter enemies for centuries.

The same thing happens today. Rather than patiently listening to and learning from those who question their beliefs - letting the debate naturally run its course to see if the challenges hold up – religious leaders often become defensive. They oversimplify and take extreme positions that appeal to their base.

Religion seems to always need an enemy to thrive, so leaders manufacture those enemies and create the war like atmosphere described above.

According to the Bible, Jesus warned against trying to separate weeds from wheat. He said "let them grow together and the angels will separate them at the end of the age." He taught people not to judge and warned that a house divided cannot stand. I can't remember a time when our society was more divided than it is now. Again, much of the blame can be placed on religion. It's time to break free.

Religious Dishonesty

"Three things cannot be long hidden: the sun, the moon, and the truth."
Gautama Buddha

Not only is religion divisive, religion is also dishonest.
There's so much to cover here. Thousands of books have been written documenting religious dishonesty, especially in Christianity. Due to the fact that the United States remains a highly religious country, we cannot achieve freedom without confronting religious dishonesty.

Many of you have already freed yourself from religion. Still, you have family and friends who have not. Hopefully, this section will help you better understand their oppression, and perhaps give you insights that will help them.

Others of you still consider yourself religious, but you also have nagging doubts. My story parallels your story in many ways. Hopefully, you're not afraid to occasionally think outside the box. You realize how susceptible we all are to religious brainwashing and psychological manipulation.

Please consider the next several sections of this book with an honest and open mind. Remember the words of Jesus in the Bible. "The truth will set you free."

Before I continue, I need to make a crucial point. Please allow me to distinguish between the institutional church and the people who support it for various reasons.

Today, I cherish the memories of many wonderful people for whom I was privileged to serve as their pastor. As is always the case, they taught and strengthened me as much as I them, if not more. I remain in contact with many of them, and it's encouraging to me that our ongoing relationship seems to outweigh our religious (and political) differences. I trust our friendship will also survive this very honest book.

I also need to distinguish between institutional religion and all the wonderful, life changing experiences people have in churches. People do have deep and often unexplainable experiences of love, healing, peace, forgiveness and support in the context of religion. It's natural to describe these experiences using religious words.

It's also natural to associate these experiences with the religious people, places and traditions they were involved in when they occurred. I am not in any way trying to diminish or lessen the value or the reality of these experiences.

I am, however, questioning the assumption that these experiences were religious experiences and could only have taken place in a religious context. People all over the world have the same experiences. They are invaluable and undeniable, but they are also universal.

If you were born and raised in India or China, rather than America, you would most likely attribute these experiences to Krishna or Buddha, rather than Jesus. Separating these experiences from religion will not diminish them in any way. It will actually make them more valuable and meaningful.

Three Big Lies

At least in the United States, and especially in more rural areas of the United States, there are three major religious lies used to exploit people. Not just in the US, but around the world, conservative Christianity - especially evangelical Christianity - exploits billions by lying about the authority of the **Bible**, the concept of **sin**, and **Jesus** himself.

For billions who call themselves "Christians", the Bible is being used to enslave them rather than set them free. Secondly, the primitive concept of sin is being used to make people feel guilty and afraid. Finally, Jesus, himself, has been replaced with a "Church" Jesus who is more an "anti-Jesus" or "anti-Christ" than the real Jesus of history.

In the following pages, I may at times get more technical than the average Christian reader is used to. I do so because I want to help, not just the typical "believer" find freedom, but also my fellow ministers. My hope is that they, like Jesus, will ultimately wake up and do their part in "setting the captives free".

So take a deep breath and try to keep an open mind during this roller coaster ride across the challenging landscape of oppressive and dishonest Christianity.

The Bible

"I do not feel obliged to believe that the same God who has endowed us with sense, reason, and intellect has intended us to forgo their use,"
Galileo Galilei

The Bible and Stages of Spiritual Maturity

Life is a journey. We all know that, but too many refuse to keep moving forward. They want to stay where they are, or even worse, move backward. Life is a wonderful, beautiful, mysterious, adventurous and scary series of changes. You will change, regardless of whether you want to or not. The question is whether you will move in the direction of truth and freedom or remain enslaved and exploited.

Consider how the Bible itself changed over time. Traditional views of the Bible completely miss this. They insist that every book in the Bible is of equal value. They refuse to acknowledge, for example, that newer parts of the Bible written closer to the time of Jesus have greater value than older parts of the Bible written during less evolved periods of human history. This dishonest approach to the Bible allows religious leaders to exploit the Bible in subtle, yet horrible ways.

Law and Rules

The first section of the Bible contains the 10 commandments, the Levitical Law, the story of Abraham, the story of how Moses delivered the Hebrews from slavery in Egypt, and the history of Israel under various kings.

The emphasis is on laws and rules. The goal is to bring order out of chaos. Violence was the norm 3000 years ago, so strict limits had to be set. Clear rules and laws had to be established.

This stage corresponds to human childhood, when rules and limits must be imposed. Children are not mature enough to make responsible decisions on their own, so they need the safety of rules and boundaries. 3000 years ago, human civilization was in its infancy and it needed rules, even ones that were far from perfect. But children grow up, human societies evolve and so did the Bible.

Incidentally, this early section of the Bible is where you find God commanding Israel to invade Jericho and kill every man, woman and child. Far too many modern Christians believe "God" actually commanded that. Why? "Because it's in the Bible." Some may even use it to justify similar atrocities today. When the masses believe such outrageous claims because "the Bible says so", the dangers of religion become obvious.

Sadly, they fail to understand that these early Biblical writings reflect the worldview of a primitive, immature human culture – not God. Or, at least, not the God that Jesus presented 1000 years later.

These early Biblical writings also contain the stories of creation and Noah's ark. These stories should be seen for what they are: ancient myths that, while they may contain value, should never be taken literally or be allowed to challenge modern science.

Prophets, Self-criticism, Limits of the Law

Over time, the rules, laws and institutions they spawned began to show wear and tear. Their limitations became obvious. Those in power ignored them, but still used them to manipulate the masses. The letter of the law was exploited, while the spirit of the law was ignored.

This paved the way for the second major section of the Bible - the prophets. The prophets were people like Elijah, Isaiah and Jeremiah, who rose up and spoke truth to power. Kings were challenged and priests were rebelled against. Hypocrisy was called out.

Most prophets were persecuted and killed by the "powers that be", but their message endured. As a result, many were set free from oppressive institutions and outdated traditions. Jesus seems to have received much of his wisdom and freedom from this section of the Bible.

This stage corresponds to late teens and early adulthood, when the rules and limits of childhood are out grown and seen for what they are. Rules for minors are well intended and necessary for a while, but they are not sufficient for the complications of adult life.

New wine demands new wineskins. Adults who remain at the level of laws and rules will be constantly frustrated, as the black and white morality that used to work so well, no longer does.

Young adults who rebel against simplistic and outdated rules and laws will obviously be a threat to the institutions that depend on them. Their questions and challenges may result in various levels of persecution, but that too is part of the journey.

Wisdom, Grace, Love, Trust

The last sections of the Old Testament and much of the New Testament, particularly the core teachings of Jesus, contain a level of freedom and wisdom not found in earlier parts of the Bible. A few basic principles replace hundreds of outdated rules and traditions.

Unconditional love, radical forgiveness and unlimited generosity carry the day. To paraphrase Jesus, "Loving your neighbor as yourself replaces all previous laws and fulfills all that the prophets foretold." The emphasis now is on healing rather than punishment, unity rather than division, compassion rather than condemnation.

Jesus was not a Pharisee or a priest. He was clearly a prophet and teacher of wisdom. He boldly challenged the earlier parts of the Bible. He identified with outcasts and sinners, rather than religious institutions. He triggered a non-violent revolution based on love. And, like so many prophets before and after, he was killed by those in power.

It's interesting to note that the latter parts of the New Testament reflect somewhat of a relapse back into rules and laws. A few generations after Jesus, institutional religion again raised its ugly head and began to water down the radical freedom that Jesus embodied. Not surprisingly, the new Christian religion quickly became just as oppressive and exploitive as the Jewish religion Jesus had rebelled against.

The powers that be – religious, political or economic – will always find a way to oppress people again and again. It's happening today. This realization led Thomas Jefferson to suggest that society needs a revolution every few generations if it is to remain free. Thank goodness, modern prophets like Gandhi and Martin Luther King, following the example of Buddha and Jesus, have shown us these revolutions need not be violent.

Where are you on your journey? Trapped in rules? Asking hard questions? Discovering a higher wisdom and freedom? After Moses and the Hebrew slaves left the bondage of Egypt and entered into the wilderness that would ultimately lead to the "Promised Land", many wanted to return to the security and familiarity of their previous slavery. Freedom can be scary, but remaining a slave is not the answer.

A Valuable Collection of Writings or Infallible Word Of God?

It's time to be honest. It's time to say what countless Christian ministers know to be true, but are afraid to say. The Bible is a valuable collection of literature. It can and has set people free. But in numerous places, the Bible reflects the primitive and crude ideas of a less civilized world. And these archaic beliefs are often used to manipulate and exploit unsuspecting and vulnerable people.

Again, I could write hundreds of pages on this topic alone, but I will limit myself. At least in the Southern and Midwestern United States, the main tool used to exploit people religiously is the Bible. Rather than just letting it be the valuable piece of literature that it is, conservative Christian leaders insist that it be viewed as "The Word of God".

They use terms such as "infallible" or "inerrant", which is the belief commonly held among fundamentalist and evangelical Christians that the Bible contains no errors. They dogmatically insist that the Biblical writers, all who happen to be men, were somehow possessed by God in such a way that their words were not their own words, but the words of God. They insist that every word, in every section of the Bible, is historically, scientifically and morally true.

The following section is written primarily for those who believe the Bible to be divinely inspired and without error. If you are among the millions who do not have this unfortunate view of the Bible, feel free to skip forward to the sections about sin and Jesus. But if you hold this view or know those who do, I believe you will find the following pages enlightening.

Not a Biblical Idea

There are numerous problems with how most conservative Christians view the Bible. First, here's what the Bible says about itself. In 2 Timothy 3:16, Paul wrote, "All Scripture is **God-breathed** and is **useful** for teaching, rebuking, correcting and training in righteousness." Notice there is no mention of "inerrancy" or "infallibility". The key word is "useful", a far softer and more humble word.

The other key word used by Paul is "God-breathed", sometimes translated "inspired". This word implies a value beyond ordinary writings, but there is nothing in the word "inspired" that implies perfection or absence of error.

In fact, the same idea of "God-breathed" occurs in Genesis 3 when God created the first man and woman. Clearly, their special place in creation did not imply perfection or complete freedom from error. We humans are neither perfect nor free from making mistakes, but we are "God-breathed" or "inspired", according to the Bible.

Another passage often quoted in defense of inerrancy is 2 Peter 1:21. It reads, "For prophecy never had its origin in the human will, but prophets, though human, spoke from God as they were carried along by the Holy Spirit."

Interestingly, if either of the above quoted words were written by Paul and Peter as most evangelical Christians claim, the "scriptures" they refer to are the Jewish scriptures which make up the Bible's Old Testament. Most of the Bible's New Testament had not yet been written.

Actually, most scholars do not believe Paul or Peter wrote these particular books. Both 2 Timothy and 2 Peter are among the last writings of the Bible, where the institutional church is beginning to water down the radically free teachings of Jesus. These books were written by disciples of Paul and Peter after they had died. Their names were attached to give them more authority, which was a common practice in ancient times. One can clearly see the institutional church beginning to control and oppress.

The waters muddy quickly as one digs deeper. Arguments for the Bible being some kind of divine revelation do not stand up to serious inquiry, even among most modern Christian scholars.

Importantly, Jesus himself challenges the idea of Biblical inerrancy in several places. In the Sermon on the Mount, Jesus repeated several times, "You have heard it said…but I say to you…" When he said, "You have heard it said," he is quoting the earliest sections of the Bible (Laws and Rules). When he then says, "but I say to you", he corrects the older teaching of scripture, replacing it with new truth.

Obviously, Jesus did not view the "Bible" he used – the Christian Old Testament - as divine revelation. According to the Bible, Jesus said, "The Spirit (not a book) will guide you to all truth."

A final scripture that many wrongly use to support inerrancy is Revelation 22:18-19. It reads, "I warn everyone who hears the words of the prophecy of this book: If anyone adds anything to them, God will add to him the plagues described in this book. And if anyone takes words away from this book of prophecy, God will take away from him his share in the tree of life and in the holy city, which are described in this book."

Many mistakenly read these words as referring to the Bible as a whole rather than just the book of Revelation. However, when John wrote Revelation, the Bible, particularly the New Testament, did not exist in its present form. That would not happen until 200 years later at the Council of Nicaea. Still, one can see why a power hungry church included it as the last book in the Bible, just in case anyone should ever question their version of Jesus or their version of "God's Word."

A Modern Invention

Most respected Christian leaders throughout history did not view the Bible the way modern evangelical Christians do. As late as the 15th century, Martin Luther and other Protestants questioned whether the books of James, Hebrews, Jude and Revelation should even be included in the New Testament; and whether the Book of Esther should be included in the Old Testament since it never mentions God.

Even today, there remains debate as to what particular books should be included in the Bible. Catholics and Episcopalians include 7 books in the Old Testament that most Protestants reject.

It's interesting that the "Bible" used by Jesus, which was a Greek translation of the Hebrew Bible (the Christian Old Testament), is not considered a very good translation by most Biblical scholars. The Septuagint, as it's called, was used by most early Christians and is the translation used when the Old Testament is quoted in the New Testament. If you look up these Old Testament quotations in a modern Bible, you will quickly notice major differences. These inaccuracies and imperfections were never an issue throughout most of Christian history.

Biblical Inerrancy was never taught during the first 1800 years of Christianity. While it may have been discussed occasionally, it only became a major issue among evangelicals during the latter part of the 20th century, due to the growing conflict between science and traditional church doctrine.

Many church leaders felt threatened by new discoveries in science, psychology and anthropology. As noted above, they began making extreme and simplistic statements that ignored the legitimate questions being raised. Those raising the questions, rather than being patiently listened to, were quickly demonized and attacked.

In his 1978 book entitled *The Battle for the Bible*, long time editor of the conservative magazine, Christianity Today, Harold Lindsell, asserted that without the doctrine of inerrancy, the church itself would unravel. It might, but so what?

Other conservative scholars like Norman Geisler of Southern Evangelical Seminary near Charlotte, North Carolina and Daniel B. Wallace of Dallas Theological Seminary in Dallas, Texas, as well as popular Southern Baptist pastor and author from Dallas, Texas, W.A. Criswell, continued to popularize inerrancy. Soon, an entire generation of conservative evangelical pastors and leaders were converted. From those fairly recent innovations, an entire shift in how millions of American Christians view the Bible took place. The debate is still going on between evangelical and mainline churches, even spilling over into politics and numerous other dimensions of public life.

I was one of those young evangelical pastors. As a young Southern Baptist minister in both Texas and Georgia, I spent many years defending (while privately questioning) an "inerrant" approach to the Bible. The older I got and the more I studied, the more problems and inconsistencies I saw. Finally, it became undeniably clear to me that inerrancy could not stand up under intense scrutiny.

Nor was it ultimately valuable. It allowed me to "preach with more authority" when I quoted from it a lot – as long as I knew which parts to focus on and which parts to avoid. More often than not, however, it became a source of conflict due to different preachers and different branches of Christianity focusing on different scriptures.

Southern Baptists experienced significant fighting and division during the 1990s, and inerrancy was a major issue. How often I wished during those years that this modern heresy of Biblical inerrancy had never raised its ugly head.

It Doesn't Work

Inerrancy does not accomplish what its proponents seek. The Bible is composed of 66 books (73 if you're Catholic or Anglican), written by perhaps 40 different (male) authors, over a period of up to 1500 years, representing various cultures and at least 3 different languages. To interpret every verse (over 30,000 in all) in a way that never contradicts any other verse requires some extremely sophisticated and highly implausible linguistic and theological gymnastics.

It's like taking 66 picture puzzles portraying different scenes and attempting to combine them all into one large puzzle. It may work in many places, but will ultimately produce a picture with numerous distortions and conflicts. It will certainly not match the beautiful gallery produced when each picture is allowed to stand on its own, and perhaps even correct inaccurate elements in the other pictures.

Allowing contradictions and errors ultimately adds to the overall value of the Bible, revealing both its frailty and its inspiration at the same time. When we insist that every verse be "perfect", we make the Bible less than what it might be when approached honestly.

An inerrant Bible does not guarantee truth. An inerrant Bible would also require an inerrant interpretation, which would also require an inerrant interpreter, and so on. Although many preachers and denominations claim to have the "true" interpretation of the Bible, how can anyone know?

A Bible which allows its less worthy parts to be judged by its more worthy parts is far more valuable than a legalistic document which refuses to be informed by honest scholarship and sound reason. Bottom line, inerrancy is a key component of religious dishonesty and exploitation.

Why Inerrancy?

I've heard many Christians say, "I would rather get to heaven and hear God say I took the Bible too seriously than to say I didn't take it seriously enough." Actually, the same thing could be said regarding the Lord's Supper, prayer, helping the poor or any number of religious activities.

But, more to the point, defending inerrancy does not necessarily mean we take the Bible more seriously, especially when it comes to living its precepts. In fact, arguments over inerrancy often distract from more important issues and help justify attitudes and behaviors that clearly contradict the core teachings of Jesus.

Why do some Christians defend inerrancy so passionately? There are several reasons. Some see the Bible as a foundation within which the least crack will continue to grow until the entire foundation crumbles. They see how science and psychology are gradually chipping away at outdated religious ideas. They are afraid of what might happen when a book they have invested so much faith in proves to be far less perfect than they once believed. Needing the Bible to be inerrant is more about egos and belief systems than it is about truth.

Actually, the Bible's errors do not take away from the Bible's truths. It doesn't make sense for anyone who believes in God to think that God cannot use a Bible that's not perfect. After all, they believe God uses imperfect people all the time. Consider the way thousands of Christians defend their support of Donald Trump.

A second reason some Christians defend Biblical inerrancy is their inability to accept the mystery and the evolving nature of existence. They desire completeness and finality. They're not comfortable with gray areas and fuzzy truths. They want the Bible to provide the answer to every question right now. It doesn't and it can't.

Whatever the word "God" points to is far bigger than any book; but many prefer the simplicity of a "God" who can be fully described in a book. Life is a journey; and while the Bible may be a valuable part of the journey for many, it should never be viewed as the full and final authority.

A third reason many Christians believe in inerrancy is because they need physical expressions of God. For some it was an idol made from wood or stone. For others it was a particular place like a mountain top, temple or place of sacrifice. For others it may be bread and wine. For still others it may be a saintly person. For many evangelicals, it seems to be the Bible.

Religious symbols may be valuable for some people's spiritual growth, but they become dangerous when taken literally. They descend into superstition and delusion. They end up sabotaging the good effect they might have otherwise had.

Fourthly, many Christian leaders worry that the average Christian will abuse a Bible with acknowledged errors, conveniently placing what they don't like in the "error" category. I'm sure they will and always have, but inerrancy does not prevent that. People accomplish the same thing by simply interpreting the Bible in ways that suit them. As stated earlier, an inerrant Bible would demand an inerrant interpreter, and so on.

Finally, and sadly, many Christian leaders are concerned about their careers. Unfortunately, they've built their entire ministries around the Bible. They preach from it every Sunday morning and base their worldview on it. To admit that the Bible has errors would be devastating to both their egos and their livelihood. Most evangelical preachers are sincere, but they are still wrong. Biblical inerrancy is a lie that allows religion to keep exploiting and enslaving millions.

Inerrancy Encourages Hate & Violence

Here's the main problem with viewing the Bible as "The Infallible or Inerrant Word of God." As suggested earlier, lies regarding the authority of the Bible are easily exploited and used to justify evil ends. How many savage wars have been fought with Biblical support from stories in the Old Testament that portray God as an angry king commanding Israel to destroy their enemies, even down to innocent children and animals? How many innocent men and women have been tortured and killed throughout history by "Bible believing" and "Bible quoting" Christians?

More recently, how many American Christians defended slavery and fought against civil rights using Biblical passages that clearly supported their positions? How often is capital punishment and other acts of violence, given added support by quoting verses from the Bible that also support capital punishment and violence - even though they also contradict the central teachings of Jesus? How many times have Christians justified not helping the poor by simply quoting the words of Jesus, "the poor are with you always", with no consideration of all the other things Jesus said about our responsibility toward the poor, and the dangers of greed?

How many conservative Christians today, rather than looking to biology and psychology, base their entire argument against gay marriage on a few verses in the Bible that condemn homosexual acts? How many churches today will not allow women to serve as priests or pastors because of a few verses in the Bible supposedly written by Paul. I say supposedly, because in another place Paul wrote "in Christ, there is no longer male nor female."

Without getting into the historical, psychological, political and theological complexities of all these issues, my point is simply that the Bible is too often used to defend overly simplistic or extreme positions that, not only contradict the teachings of Jesus, but also ignore credible science and history, as well as ignore basic human rights. Belief in inerrancy not only makes this easy to do, it often makes it unavoidable.

Are There Errors and Contradictions in the Bible?

Are there errors and contradictions in the Bible? Of course there are. For anyone who takes the teachings of Jesus seriously, the parts of the Bible that contradict his fundamental emphasis on love, compassion and grace, must be rejected. For example, Old Testament scriptures depicting a vengeful, jealous and cruel God are obvious errors.

Biblical inerrancy encourages images of God and views of reality that are irresponsible, mean spirited and dangerous - images that clearly betray the teachings of Jesus. Much of what the New Testament teaches about God's anger and wrath reflects human anger and wrath - not the God of Jesus who loved unconditionally and showed infinite mercy.

Any part of the Bible that contradicts obvious scientific truth is an error. The universe is obviously billions of years old, not thousands. While numerous Christian schools refuse to teach evolution, the universe keeps evolving.

When the Bible says one thing in one place and something different in another place - at least one of those places contains error. For example, there are many details about Jesus' trial and crucifixion in John that contradict Matthew, Mark and Luke. I have listed several of these in the appendix. The birth lineage of Jesus in Matthew contradicts the one in Luke.

Conservative Christian preachers know this, but seldom talk about it. When they do, they try to explain it away with arguments that sound more like political spin than honest dialogue.

Here's the reality of the situation. The Bible is a valuable collection of early Christian writings approved by church bishops 300 years after Jesus died. There were many early Christian writings the bishops decided not to include.

The bishop of Rome obviously had more influence than other bishops, due to the fact that the Roman Emperor had recently made Christianity the official religion of the Roman Empire. So in addition to sincere spiritual motives, there were powerful political forces at work also.

To ignore the above reality and claim that the Bible is "God's Word" is naïve at best. But more than that, it handicaps one's pursuit of truth and keeps one enslaved to a religious system that has manipulated and exploited the masses for centuries. It continues allowing powerful people and institutions to perform horrendous acts of evil in the name of God.

According to the Bible, Jesus promised that "the Spirit (not a book) would guide you to all truth." Open your eyes and heart, and be free!

John Alan Shope

Sin

"There's no problem so awful, that you can't add some guilt to it and make it even worse," Bill Watterson

Guilt and Punishment

Now let's turn to religion's second major lie. Most conservative religions, especially evangelical Christianity, start with the assumption that all humans are sinful, guilty and depraved. What logically follows is that people deserve to be punished because of this.

Of course, religion then comes in to save the day by offering forgiveness, salvation and hope. This entire paradigm is dishonest and exploitive.

It's similar to the "good cop" / "bad cop' routine often used by police to get criminals to confess crimes. Only this time, the people being targeted are not criminals. They're innocent children and vulnerable adults.

Let me share an analogy to show how religion uses the concept of sin to make people feel guilty, and then exploits that guilt. When a child experiences pain and suffering at the hands of a parent, the child naturally thinks she/he is at fault and is being punished for doing something wrong. The child is completely innocent, but still must rationalize the pain; and does so by blaming herself/himself. Sadly, this is a natural human response that occurs repeatedly in abusive situations.

Christianity does the same thing on a more massive scale. The world is full of pain and death. Human suffer repeatedly in large and small ways. It is a natural human response, especially in religious cultures, to wonder if we are being punished by God. It is extremely easy for charismatic religious leaders to exploit this and convince us that we are.

Viewing the Bible as "God's Holy Word" enforces such dishonesty. According to the first pages of the Bible, Adam and Eve disobeyed God in the Garden of Eden. As a result, pain and death entered the world. Humans continue to disobey, and the world continues to suffer. It's our fault that we suffer as much as we do.

To drive their point home, preachers quote other verses from the Bible: "All have sinned and fallen short of the glory of God." "There is none righteous, no, not one." "All our righteous acts are like a filthy rag." "I was born in sin."

Sadly, in the same way that many Muslims are exploited by the Quran, many Christians believe that to question the Bible is to question God.

Finally, we are told, not only does God punish us here, but we will spend eternity in hell if we don't accept God's salvation and forgiveness by "accepting Jesus as Lord and Savior" or by being baptized or by doing whatever else our particular church or religion tells us to do.

To make matters worse, blame and punishment become the norm in our societies. God blames and punishes us, so we feel justified in blaming and punishing each other. People become like their "God".

Thankfully, more and more people are realizing that this whole concept of sin and punishment is dishonest, exploitive and cruel. How wonderful it is when an abused child finally grows up and realizes that all the pain and suffering was not his or her fault. The parent was sick in some way, or something else was going on that the child could not see or understand. The child suffered as a result, but it was never the child's fault.

Our world is full of pain and death. Religion has always tried to explain why, but none of the answers satisfy. We don't know why we live in a universe that can be so painful. But we should know this: It is not our fault. You and I are not being punished.

I'm not talking about facing the consequences of actions that are clearly dangerous and risky. We are all broken and blind, and we all do things that cause ourselves and others pain. We need to be healed and educated, perhaps even isolated and quarantined at times.

But we never need to be punished. The whole concept of punishment is childish and misguided. It only makes a bad situation worse. It only makes broken people more broken and angry.

Stop punishing yourself and others. Is there a place for self defense and imprisonment? Yes. We have to protect ourselves and our loved ones from broken and blind people. But prisons should be about public safety, education and healing - not punishment.

I spent 20 years working in the criminal justice system. Decades of research have been conducted regarding the best way to treat those who break our laws and threaten our safety. Punishment doesn't work. It may make us feel better, but it only creates more hardened criminals.

What works is to discover why people commit criminal acts, and then try to prevent it. Some people are broken beyond repair and should never be released from incarceration. But the motive should be public safety, not punishment.

In 1966, Charles Whitman, a young ex-marine, killed his mother, his wife and 14 others in Austin, Texas. He was ultimately killed by police officers. In a note left behind, he asked doctors to do an autopsy on his brain and try to understand the rage he was feeling. The autopsy found a large tumor in his brain that could easily explain his actions. Could he help what he did? Did he freely choose to kill those people? Had he lived, should he have been punished?

This is a rather extreme example, but to a lesser degree, all our actions – good and bad – are driven by neurotransmitters in our brain reacting to random events in our environment over a long period of time. Some brains work better than others. Some brains are severely broken. His obviously was. Had he lived, he would obviously need surgery and quarantine perhaps, but not punishment.

Substitutionary Atonement

Unfortunately, those who believe that God gets angry and punishes us will find it easy to justify their own anger and desire to punish. They will also find it easy to believe one of the most dangerous Christian lies of all related to sin: the claim that Jesus "died for our sins". While "dying for our sins" could be interpreted in several ways, evangelical Christianity usually understands it as "Substitutionary Atonement".

"Substitutionary Atonement" is the fundamentalist Christian idea that God punished Jesus on the cross, so that he would not have to punish us. The story goes like this. God is love, but God is also holy. We deserve eternal separation from God in hell, but Jesus took our place. If we simply trust what Jesus did and accept him as our Lord and Savior, our sins will be forgiven and we will go to heaven when we die. However, those who do not trust solely in Jesus' act of "Substitutionary Atonement" will not be saved and will spend eternity in hell.

Interestingly, trying to be good may actually be a bad thing in the mind of many evangelical Christians; because it may indicate that you are not completely trusting Jesus alone for your salvation. In a subtle way, this can make it easier to overlook inappropriate behavior and write it off as normal and expected. After all, what more should we expect from "sinful" and "fallen" human beings?

My point is we need to re-examine the whole concept of "sin" and "punishment". Letting go of unhealthy and irrational views of the Bible allows us to do this. If anything, sin is brokenness that needs healing – not a crime that needs avenging. Sinners are blind people who need to be enlightened - not criminals who need to be punished.

Like many of those who speak truth to power, Jesus died at the hands of a religious and political system that felt deeply threatened by his revolutionary ideas and his popularity among the people. The idea that Jesus was punished by God in our place is a silly idea with roots in Greek mythology – not the teachings of Jesus.

"Substitutionary Atonement", like several other Christian ideas related to Jesus, has parallels in Greek Mystery religions which were popular during the time Jesus. A generation later, this particular myth was used to explain why God allowed Jesus to die so horribly. Ultimately, this myth became extremely valuable to institutional Christianity in that it gave the church something to offer the masses in return for their allegiance and support.

It also allowed religious leaders to interpret, control and broker a theological mechanism which determined one's eternal destiny. Talk about power! Sadly, millions still believe it today and are unwittingly exploited by it.

Hell

Let me briefly address the concept of hell, which obviously stems from the traditional Christian dogma that we are all sinners, and that a "holy" God has no choice but to punish us for all eternity.

Like other religious symbols, the word "hell" might have value if it were not taken literally. "Having hell to pay" would mean the same as "reaping what one sows". The Hindu concept of karma is a similar idea. A more modern expression might be "what goes around comes around".

In other words, "hell" is not about eternal judgment. "Hell" is what we do to ourselves and each other every day when we act selfishly and ignorantly. We all do better when we all do better. But when we take our individuality to an extreme, and become addicted to selfish pleasures, "hell on earth" is the result.

In our self-centered isolation, we lose our compassion for others and become cold and greedy. Dying to self and living as one with the rest of humanity is the only way to turn "hell" into "heaven". Hopefully, our species is evolving in that direction.

Unfortunately, most conservative religions, especially evangelical Christianity, interpret "hell" literally. Such primitive thinking is hypocritical, illogical and just another tool to scare and exploit vulnerable people. For many, a belief in hell simply reflects their own desire to punish rather than forgive.

In defense of a literal hell, some Christians will quote verses from the Bible which depict Jesus as warning about hell. First, it's naïve to think that Jesus actually said everything the Bible claims. The earliest gospels were written at least a generation after his death.

Secondly, even if he did use the word "hell", the actual word in the original Greek manuscripts is "Gehenna", and it refers to a well known landfill outside Jerusalem which was always burning. Obviously, Jesus could have used the word metaphorically to refer to wasted lives or painful regrets. It's doubtful Jesus ever used it to refer to a place of eternal punishment.

For what it's worth, there are just as many verses in the Bible that challenge the concept of a literal eternal hell as there are verses that support it. Universalism, the idea that God will ultimately reconcile all things to himself, has been expounded by Christian leaders from the beginning of the church. The problem is that early Christian leaders who rejected the concept of a literal hell were never in the majority; and the majority obviously found literal ideas of hell more valuable to institutional survival.

Finally, from a theological perspective (assuming one cares about theology), it doesn't make sense for a loving and gracious God to have created a world in which some of God's creation would remain in darkness and pain forever. Creation itself should be seen as an act of love and generosity - not a test that some of God's creatures will pass while others fail.

As suggested by Richard Rohr, who was a tremendous help in my own journey to freedom, "If just one soul ends up in hell, then God loses and the devil wins."[2] Richard is speaking of the devil metaphorically of course.

Richard goes on to question how Jesus could ask us to forgive unconditionally if God does not forgive unconditionally. That would make us more loving and gracious than God! We are asked to forgive rather than punish, yet God punishes us (or he punishes Jesus in our

---

[2] From a 2015 lecture by Richard Rohr entitled, "Hell, No!"

place).

The whole concept of hell and punishment is theologically inconsistent and completely out of harmony with the teachings of Jesus. This is the main reason liberal religion and liberal Christianity stopped believing in concepts like hell and Jesus dying on the cross for our sins many generations ago. You should, too. Be free!

John Alan Shope

Jesus

"We can easily forgive a child who is afraid of the dark; the real tragedy of life is when men are afraid of the light," Plato

Now it's time to consider perhaps the cruelest and most blasphemous religious lie of all. It has to do with the person of Jesus. According to the Christian Bible, Jesus once asked, "Who do men say that I am?" Just like today, there were many different opinions as to who Jesus was. In another place, he warned his followers, "People will say to you, 'Look! There he is!' or 'Look! Here he is!' But don't go and chase after him." Good advice.

The more knowledge you have of history, particularly Christian history, the more you are forced to question the traditional image of Jesus. Hundreds of previously unknown Christian writings have been discovered during the past 75 years, beginning with the Nag Hammadi and Dead Sea Scrolls in the 1940s. Many of these were only published in the 1990s due to conflicts over ownership. They clearly challenge the traditional image of Jesus set forth by the church.

Most of the information contained in these documents has not yet filtered down to the average Christian. Part of this is obviously due to strong resistance from conservative Christian scholars, who rightly see these documents as a threat to their own traditional views of Jesus. Another reason is that people in general simply do not read as much as they used to - which raises other concerns beyond the scope of this book.

The descriptions of Jesus contained in these hundreds of documents vary greatly. Many are obvious fiction, while others contain information every bit as credible as documents included in the Christian Bible. What they clearly show is that early Christians did not agree on who Jesus was, nor did they agree on what he did or said. Different regions of the early Christian world had very different versions of Jesus.

To show how divided the early Christians were, a document written by Irenaeus of Lyons 150 years after Jesus' death was entitled "Against Heresies". Irenaeus is condemning other versions of Jesus as heresies. The reason we still have his writings and not the so called "heretical" ones is because Irenaeus represented what later became the "official" version of Jesus, and it's always the winners who write history. Thankfully, some of the other versions of Jesus are now showing up in the aforementioned Nag Hammadi and Dead Sea Scrolls.

The Evolution of Jesus

All religions evolve over time. Jesus himself never wrote anything down, nor did his earliest followers, most of whom could not read or write. Our earliest information about Jesus was preserved in oral, rather than written form. Only after the first followers of Jesus began to die, did the next generation of followers begin to write down what they had heard from Jesus' first followers. This gap of around 50 years between the death of Jesus and the first written records resulted in many different versions of Jesus.

Interestingly, while the Christian New Testament was originally written in Greek, Jesus and his first disciples spoke Aramaic, which opened up even more opportunities for different versions of Jesus to emerge.

Regional versions of Jesus continued to evolve and grow more diverse over the next 300 years. By 325 AD, Christianity was a much divided religion with many different worldviews. Every group had their own set of "official" writings and traditions, all claiming to stem from Jesus' first disciples.

Most agreed that Jesus was an enlightened religious reformer whose teachings challenged the religious and political powers of his day. Most also saw him as a miracle worker and healer who dramatically changed the lives of numerous individuals.

But some began to draw from other religions that were popular at the time and claim that Jesus was much more than just a teacher and a healer. One can easily trace Jesus' evolution from "Son of Man" to "Son of God" in the New Testament. (See the appendix.)

Greco-Roman Mystery Religions

Greco-Roman Mystery religions greatly influenced early Christianity and its evolving perceptions of Jesus. The Mystery religions had been around for centuries, and remained extremely popular in the Greek and Roman world of the 2nd and 3rd centuries. Their beliefs and practices stemmed from much earlier tribal religions. The similarities between them and Christianity are interesting to say the least.

For example, some of the mystery religions celebrated a ritual meal on a regular basis, through which the participants became one with a particular deity. Most admitted new members through a ritual bath or baptism. Several believed in a god-man who died, descended into hell, and was then resurrected. A miraculous birth was another common element in many of the stories. Some had a goddess or mother weeping over the death of her half-god son. **Again, all these stories pre-date the birth of Jesus.**

Christian missionaries, especially Roman Catholics, have always drawn from the local customs and beliefs of new converts. Most current Christian holidays are actually pagan holidays that were subsequently given Christian meaning. As one studies the Greek Mystery religions, it becomes clear that early Christians borrowed many of their ideas about Jesus from these older religions.

In fact, the similarities were so obvious to people of the 3rd century, that one early Christian leader, Justin Martyr, had to explain the coincidence. He asserted that Satan foresaw the coming of Jesus and inspired these other religions to teach similar stories - before Jesus was born - so that people would be confused later. [3]

In spite of more historically accurate versions of Jesus still existing, the more mythical and sensational versions, heavily influenced by the Mystery religions, began to dominate.

Much of this was due to the influence of the Roman Emperor, Constantine. The more mythical version of Christianity had the same popular appeal as the Mystery religions, and also had the potential to bring all the various religions together in a more manageable way, which benefitted the Empire.

Soon, to assure a greater sense of unity and control within what was now a fully institutionalized Church, the Bishop of Rome and other like-minded Church leaders tried to suppress other versions of Jesus, including those that were historically more accurate. Ultimately, they decreed that anyone who disagreed with the official Roman version of Jesus was a "heretic" and should be banished or killed.

The "Official" Jesus

In 325 AD, almost 300 years after Jesus' death, the more mythical, Roman version of Jesus was presented to the Mediterranean world as the official version of Jesus. It was agreed upon by Christian bishops during a council convened by the Emperor Constantine in the city of Nicaea. Today, millions of Christians still recite the Nicene Creed every Sunday morning.

Here it is.

"I believe in one God, the Father Almighty, Maker of heaven and earth, and of all things visible and invisible.

And in one Lord Jesus Christ, the only-begotten Son of God, begotten of the Father before all worlds; God of God, Light of Light, very God of very God; begotten, not made, being of one substance with the Father, by

---

[3] First Apology, chapter 54, Justin Martyr, circa AD 155

whom all things were made.

Who, for us men for our salvation, came down from heaven, and was incarnate by the Holy Spirit of the virgin Mary, and was made man; and was crucified also for us under Pontius Pilate; He suffered and was buried; and the third day He rose again, according to the Scriptures; and ascended into heaven, and sits on the right hand of the Father; and He shall come again, with glory, to judge the quick and the dead; whose kingdom shall have no end."

People of that day would have quickly recognized the similarities between the Nicene Creed and popular Mystery religions. For political reasons, many Christian leaders needed Jesus to be that kind of heroic God-man. Believing in that version of Jesus soon became a test of one's loyalty both to the Bishop of Rome and to the Roman emperor.

As often happens in religion, what one believed gradually became more important than how one behaved. Many of the teachings of Jesus related to individual and social behavior took a back seat to a less demanding system of beliefs.

Over the next several generations, the more historically accurate versions of Jesus were gradually eliminated and forgotten. For the next 1700 years, there was only one version of Jesus – the Roman version. With the exception of a few "liberal" denominations, this version continues to be the "official" version of Jesus espoused by modern Christianity - Roman Catholic, Orthodox, Protestant and Evangelical.

8 Surprising Images of Jesus from the Bible.

It was also during the Council of Nicaea in 325 AD, led by the Bishop of Rome, that the Church decided which books would comprise the Christian Bible. Out of hundreds of early Christian documents related to Jesus, 39 were chosen to be the "New Testament". In this new Christian Bible, the 70 or so Jewish books that Jesus and his first followers used became the "Old Testament". Obviously, the "New Testament" supported the Roman version of Jesus because it was, for the most part, produced by Rome.

Half of the 39 New Testament books were written by Paul of Tarsus, who never actually met Jesus. He seems to have had some contact with Jesus' disciples, but most of his ideas arose from his own mystical experiences, including a mystical encounter with Jesus which led to his "Christian" conversion while traveling to Damascus. Many scholars view Paul as the true founder of Christianity, since there is little evidence that Jesus ever intended to start a religion.

Most of what the Bible teaches regarding the life of Jesus is found in the first 4 books of the New Testament. These are called the "gospels" (Matthew, Mark, Luke and John). The rest of the New Testament, the majority of which was written by Paul, is more theological and reflects issues confronting the early church.

Regarding descriptions of Jesus contained in the 4 gospels, traditional Christianity usually interprets them in a way that keeps them in harmony with the writings of Paul and the original teachings of the Roman church.

However, if one studies the 4 gospels objectively, one can still find images of a Jesus that does not match the traditional "church" Jesus. Among these scattered images, we probably see reflections of the true Jesus of history.

These occasional snapshots describe a much more "liberal" Jesus. While this version of Jesus can be found in a few liberal Christian denominations, it may come as a shock to most conservative and evangelical Christians. Here are some images of the more liberal and less mythical Jesus that can be found in the Bible when one searches honestly.

1. **Jesus was always on the side of the poor.** His teachings about the Kingdom of God were almost always tied to justice for the poor. In Matthew 25:31-46, he made helping the poor the key to entering the Kingdom of God. He said what you do or don't do for the poor is the same as what you do or don't do for him.

2. **Jesus was not a Capitalist.** In Like 18:18-30, Jesus told a rich young ruler to "sell all his possessions and give the money to the poor." Many Christians are quick to reply that Jesus only said that to one particular person. But they conveniently ignore Luke 12:32-33, where he told all his followers to "sell their possessions and give the money to the poor." Jesus said more about money than any other one topic and most of what he said was negative. He constantly warned the rich regarding money and greed.

3. **Jesus was always on the side of immigrants and foreigners.** In one of his most famous parables – the Good Samaritan – the hero was a hated foreigner (Luke 10:25-37). Several of his healings involved foreigners whom he praised for having more faith than his fellow Jews who hated them (Matthew 8:5-13, Matthew 15:21-28).

4. **Jesus never condemned homosexuality.** In fact, several scholars believe the Roman Centurion's servant he healed in Matthew 8 was actually the Centurion's male lover, based on the particular Greek word used for servant. In that day, it was commonly used to refer to same sex concubines, which was common among Roman soldiers. Jesus not only healed his partner, he commended the soldier for his faith. In a more general sense, Jesus' statement that people will not marry in the Kingdom of God points to a state of being beyond personal identities based on gender; as does Paul's statement that "in Christ, there is neither male nor female."

5. **Jesus was radical in his treatment of women.** He shocked his disciples by having a conversation with the "woman at the well" who was also a foreigner (John 4:27). After his death, the first person to experience him as still alive in some way was Mary Magdalene (John 20:11-18, Mark 16:9)). He also had women among his followers which was almost unheard of in that day (Luke 8:1-3).

6. **Jesus did not approve of war.** He said in Matthew 5:9, "Blessed are the peacemakers for they shall be called the children of God." In Matthew 26:52, he told Peter not to use his sword to protect him as he was being arrested. He added, "Those who live by the sword will die by the sword." Jesus' disciples hoped Jesus would lead a revolt against Rome, but he refused, possibly prompting his betrayal by Judas. Most modern Christian do not know that early Christians

were pacifists and that soldiers could not be part of the early church.

7. **Jesus always took the side of so called "sinners".** He defended the woman caught in adultery. He was constantly criticized for hanging out with gluttons, drunkards, prostitutes and other social outcasts. He was called a "friend of sinners" (Matthew 11:19). He seemed to enjoy parties and supposedly turned water into wine at a wedding, even after many had already become intoxicated (John 2:1-10).

8. **Jesus was critical of institutional religion.** The Pharisees, Sadducees, Priests and Levites were the religious leaders of his day. They represented the "church" of his day. Jesus was always in conflict with them and always criticizing them. He called them "whitewashed tombs" and "hypocrites" (Matthew 23:26-28, John 2:11-17). In several parables, the priests and Levites were presented as the bad guys, while the "sinners" and "foreigners" were the good guys (Luke 10:25-37, Luke 18:9-14). Jesus only mentioned hell when he was criticizing religious leaders.

While I cannot ascertain to what degree the Biblical images above reflect the true Jesus of history, they certainly call into question the typical version of Jesus offered by TV preachers and most evangelical churches. It's certainly not the "Jesus" they say you must "accept as your personal Lord and Savior" or else go to hell. So, who is the real Jesus? Can we even know?

The True Jesus of History

Again, the winners always write the history books. As already stated, the Christian church at Rome, in collusion with the Roman Emperor, Constantine, won the day regarding which version of Jesus would become the official version. With the strength of the Empire behind them, the Roman church was successful in suppressing oral traditions and destroying documents that contained a more accurate version of Jesus.

While non-Christian scholars have always questioned the traditional view of Jesus, Christian scholars began seriously questioning them in the 1800s. In the 1900s, historical and textual evidence against traditional images of Jesus became so overwhelming that some ministers and churches left traditional Christianity and gave birth to a smaller, liberal wing of Christianity that continues today.

Fortunately, for those of us seeking the truth about Jesus, even more reliable data has surfaced in recent decades due to even greater advances in textual and historical criticism and the aforementioned recent discoveries of numerous ancient documents.

When you free Jesus from the institutional church, you find a very different, but no less inspiring individual. While we still know far less than we would like to know regarding Jesus, recent efforts by groups of Biblical scholars like the Jesus Seminar[4] have made substantial progress. Based on the latest research, a more historically accurate version of Jesus probably looks something like the following.

He seems to have valued mystical experiences which often involved healings of various kinds. He may have been influenced by an ancient form of Jewish mysticism called Kabbalah. Many of his teachings share ideas with an ascetic Jewish sect known as Essenes, who lived in communes and shared all their property. He seems to have been familiar with Jewish apocalyptic ideas that were popular in his life time.

He was certainly not part of the Jewish religious or political establishment. Whether by choice or chance, he was poor and identified with outcasts and others who were socially discriminated against.

His unique speaking style, using parables and witty sayings, made him very popular among the common people and the non-religious. He was considered a "miracle worker" by many, and seems to have had a dramatic, life changing effect on a number of his followers. Many of them continued proclaiming his radical message of freedom and compassion after his death, even at the cost of their own lives.

---

[4] https://www.westarinstitute.org/projects/the-jesus-seminar/

He was a free thinker and dared to think outside the religious and political boxes of his day. During his lifetime, he boldly stood up for the poor and powerless and challenged the religious and political systems that exploited them. He drew a following, made waves and rocked boats. As so often happens to people who speak truth to power, the powers that be ultimately had him killed.

Obviously, many of his spiritual and political insights survived his martyrdom and sowed the seeds that later became part of the Christian religion. In spite of how the Christian religion and the institutional church so often betrayed him, Jesus' example and his teachings have continued to inspire numerous reformers and activists such as Mahatma Gandhi and Martin Luther King.

Finally, he is someone that many claim to have had mystical encounters with, both immediately following his death and throughout history. They claim to have received comfort, guidance and hope from him during times of personal crisis. This last claim obviously raises the question of Jesus' resurrection.

The Resurrection of Jesus

The church claims that God raised Jesus from the dead and that he appeared, in his physical body, to hundreds of people. The resurrection of Jesus lies at the foundation of traditional Christianity. Many go to church only once per year on Easter Sunday to celebrate the resurrection. Most conservative Christian scholars will assert that, without the resurrection, Christianity is meaningless. So what happened on that first Easter morning 2000 years ago?

After Jesus died, some of his followers claimed to have seen and talked to him again. The Biblical details are somewhat inconsistent and vary from some type of spiritual vision to an actual physical event.

The traditional resurrection stories presented by the church are obviously embellished. When you compare the stories in Matthew, Luke and John, there are numerous contradictions, which suggest that the original stories evolved quite a bit prior to being written down. (See examples in the appendix.)

Interestingly, in the oldest copies of the book of Mark, which is the earliest of the 4 Biblical gospels, there is no encounter with the risen Jesus. Mary Magdalene and two other women find an empty tomb and a young man dressed in white, who tells them Jesus has been raised. The current story found in Mark was added many years later, along with other verses that are obvious additions. Most modern Bibles even admit this in a footnote.

Some historians suggest that someone either misplaced or stole Jesus' body, leading to early stories of an empty tomb, which only later evolved into stories of a resurrection.

Still, there is some evidence that one or more of his followers had some kind of moving experience with what they perceived to be Jesus, shortly after his death. Mary Magdalene, a female disciple who may have actually authored one of the recently discovered Nag Hammadi scrolls, seems to have been the first to have such an experience.

Some historians suggest that the sudden boldness of his followers and their willingness to later die as martyrs is evidence for some kind of post death encounter with Jesus that one or more of his followers had experienced.

All cultures contain stories of post death encounters with loved ones and others. According to the Bible, not only Jesus, but Moses, Samuel and Elijah also appeared to certain people after they had died.

Throughout history, numerous people claim to have had so called "Christic visions". I personally know two women alive today who claim to have encountered Jesus during a time of personal crisis. I cannot easily dismiss their claims.

Their dramatic encounter with Jesus is similar to others who have had post death encounters with deceased loved ones. Such encounters often take away people's fear of death and provide a new sense of peace and hope.

This is probably the kind of experience Mary Magdalene, and perhaps others, had with Jesus following his crucifixion. While the church insists that the resurrection of Jesus was different and unique, this more common mystical encounter seems far more likely.

Interpreting the resurrection of Jesus in this way should not make Jesus less inspiring or less consoling to the millions who follow him. It should not diminish the peace and hope that Jesus gives so many regarding death.

In contrast, it actually presents that hope in a less sensational and more credible manner. In other words, you don't have to trust a religious institution or see a "ghost" yourself in order to believe that, perhaps, something within us survives death.

An Honest Prayer to Jesus

According to the Bible, Jesus once asked his disciples "Who do men say I am?" After listening to the various opinions, he then asked, "Who do you say I am?" During my years as a Christian minister, I struggled with this question. As I shared earlier, it was hard to finally let go of the church's Jesus. It was such a deep, deep part of who I was.

Throughout my struggle, I often prayed to Jesus and asked him to help me know the truth. I wrote many of these prayers in a journal. They reflect how difficult my own path to freedom was. For what it's worth, here is a montage of those prayers.

"Jesus, so many worship you and thank you for dying on a cross for their sins – allowing God to forgive their sins by punishing you in their place. Is that really true? You told people their sins were forgiven simply because God loved them unconditionally. You talked about a prodigal son whom his father gladly received back home and forgave, simply because he loved him. No one had to be punished in the son's place.

Why did the church, later on, make it all about "an eye for an eye and a tooth for a tooth" - your "eyes" and "teeth" in place of ours? You clearly said that type of thinking is wrong. Why it is so hard for us to let God love us unconditionally? Is it because we have so seldom felt unconditional love from others? Do we need to punish those who hurt us; therefore, we need a God who also punishes? It seems to be in our nature to judge and punish people - even ourselves - but that's not what you taught. Surely, that's not how God is.

I trust you, and I trust what you taught about love. I trust that I will learn from my mistakes and perhaps someday be healed from my ignorance and selfishness. I don't fear being punished by an angry and wrathful "God". I punish myself everyday by acting selfishly and ignorantly. I need healing. I trust evolution will ultimately make all of us more like you. If not, we probably won't survive as a species.

And what about the idea that God physically raised you from the dead? I believe that in some mysterious way, you are still present and perhaps hearing this prayer. Does that possibility give me hope, only if I believe what the church and the church's Bible teach about you? I, along with millions of others, occasionally feel your presence. It gives me peace and hope in the face of death. Why do I need religion or religious institutions to affirm that?

Some of your followers tell me I'm "not saved" and I'm "going to hell" because I can't accept everything the church or the church's Bible says about you. Religious people told you the same thing. I'll try to love as you loved and live as you lived; but it's a lot easier to just "believe" in you than to "follow" your example. I need your help. Amen"

If Jesus Came To Your Town Today

After decades of studying the Bible, church history and Christian theology, after providing countless hours of spiritual direction and conducting more funerals than I can remember, after a lifetime of prayer and meditation, after years of working outside the church as a counselor, criminal justice professional, researcher and writer; I am absolutely convinced, and will stake my eternal destiny on this: **the first followers of Jesus would not recognize the "Jesus" of traditional Christianity.**

Jesus, himself, would be shocked and dismayed by the religion that now bears his name. I honestly believe that if Jesus were here today, the modern church would find him just as offensive and threatening as religious leaders of his own day did. Crucifixion would not be an option today, but they would certainly declare him a heretic and attack him in every way possible.

BJ Thomas, who's religious music often colored outside traditional lines, recorded a powerful song entitled, "Would They Love Him Down in Shreveport?" The lyrics imagine what it would it be like if Jesus came to various towns in the U.S. today. Picking up on that theme, I'm convinced he would say something like the following.

"I never intended to start a new religion. I never claimed to be the "only" Son of God, or even sinless. I certainly never claimed to be the Savior of the world, or the Jewish Messiah. Religion created all this after I died.

I was a teacher, and many called me a prophet. I challenged all religion, by asserting that God loves everyone, always and forever, unconditionally. Therefore, we don't need religion or religious institutions. Everything is sacred.

The Bible does contain some of what I actually said. I did say that the Kingdom of Heaven is not in a particular place. It is spread all over the earth, but people don't see it. I did say that the Kingdom of God is within you.

My main message was that we need to forgive each other for our blindness and brokenness. We need to be content with what we have, and share everything we have. Yes, that was radical then and still is today.

I also taught that we need not be afraid of death. We can trust God or the Universe or a Higher Power. It doesn't matter what name you use.

Isn't it ironic that the church founded in my name would most likely reject me today as a heretic? Many of its leaders, while sincere, still don't know me. Others of them knowingly twist my words to fit their own selfish desires for power. Here are a few examples.

*I taught that **all people are children of God**. The church taught that only I was, and invented the doctrine of the "Trinity" and the "Virgin Birth".*

*I taught that **the Spirit of God within us will guide us to the truth**. The church taught that only certain writings and certain people could guide us, and invented the "Bible", "Ordination" and the "Priesthood".*

*I taught that **every meal should be a symbol of our oneness with each other**. The church taught that only my last meal was and invented the "Lord's Supper" or the "Eucharist"; a meal only they and people like them could participate in.*

*I taught that **God dwells within all people, and that all people are basically good**. The church taught that all people are basically bad and invented the doctrine of "Original Sin" and "Hell".*

*I taught that **we should all make sacrifices for each other**. The church taught that my sacrifice was the only one needed and invented "Substitutionary Atonement". Just believing in my sacrifice is much easier, but it won't make the world a better place. I wanted people to actually follow my example.*

*I taught **we need not fear death**. We should "die to our small "self" trusting that something bigger within us survives death in a way we don't fully understand. The church taught that my physical body actually rose from the dead and invented the idea of a "Bodily Resurrection" in "Heaven".*

*I taught that **my spirit would continue to be present on the Earth in various ways and in various people**. The church taught that I would actually return to Earth someday in physical form and invented the "Second Coming". Unfortunately, that idea encourages people to wait on me to come back and fix things, instead of trying to make the world better right now by following my teachings.*

*I taught that **God loves, forgives and accepts everyone, unconditionally**. The church taught that God accepts only certain people who believe certain things and invented "Christianity".*

Jesus and Buddha

I trust that many of you are beginning to get glimpses of a much different Jesus than the one invented and controlled by the church. Traditional Christianity presents a mythical and convoluted version of Jesus, and then threatens you with "eternal hell" for rejecting it. There are so many other, far more credible, ways to understand and even follow Jesus.

I want to close this section by suggesting an approach to understanding Jesus that I'm surprised more has not been written about. Many, me included, believe that Jesus probably had more in common with ancient Buddhism than with modern Christianity. If he were here today, I believe he would sound more like a Buddhist than a Christian. There are several compelling reasons to believe this.

Actually, a lot has been written about the similarities between Jesus and Buddha, but very little has filtered down to the average Christian. Like in the case of the Nag Hammadi and Dead Sea Scrolls, part of this is obviously due to how threatening such an idea is to modern Christianity, and to those who depend on the institution for their livelyhood. Please consider the following with an open mind and heart.

Buddha lived 500 years before Jesus. He challenged the ancient religion of Hinduism the same way Jesus challenged the ancient religion of Judaism. One of the greatest Indian emperors of all time, Ashoka, ruled over the Indian subcontinent and much of the Middle East from 268 until 232 BC. In 263 BC he converted to Buddhism. This was about 250 years after Buddha and about 250 years before Jesus.

The famous and extensively traveled "silk road", which stretched from the Korean peninsula to the Mediterranean Sea, made the exchange of ideas between the east and west inevitable. One of emperor Ashoka's most notable accomplishments was sending Buddhist missionaries across the Middle East and into the Mediterranean world. Their mission was so successful that Buddhist missionaries and Buddhist converts continued to occupy these areas for the next several hundred years. This included the region of Palestine where Jesus grew up and taught.

As Jewish author and editor Dr. S. M. Melamed stated, *"Numerous scholars long ago discovered Buddhistic elements in the Gospel of John and also recognized the Buddhistic background of Essenism, by which Jesus was greatly influenced. The conclusion is inescapable that Palestine, together with many other parts of Asia Minor, was inundated with Buddhistic propaganda for two centuries before Christ."* [5]

Some claim Jesus traveled to India during his so called "missing years" between the ages of around 12 and 30. While there is little credible evidence to support this, it is very likely that Jesus encountered Buddhist missionaries and converts in and around Palestine. The Christmas story of "the three wise men" or "magi from the east" visiting Jesus at his birth may actually stem from an encounter between an adult Jesus and Buddhist monks.

There's substantial evidence suggesting that Jesus was heavily influenced by Buddhist ideas. Many of Jesus' teachings are very similar to the teachings of Buddha. To the shock of most conservative Christians, much of what Jesus said was actually said by Buddha several hundred years before Jesus. The golden rule, dying to self, and loving your enemies were all ideas that Buddha taught long before Jesus did.

Ancient Buddhist scriptures contain stories about Buddha that are very similar to the stories we now associate with Jesus. There are ancient Buddhist stories about Buddha being born of a virgin, feeding the multitudes and walking on water. Some would argue that these stories were borrowed from stories about Jesus, but the Buddhist documents appear to pre-date the Christian documents. (See Appendix for more examples.)

Everything is Ultimately One Thing

Beyond specific stories and statements, there are also fundamental

---

[5] S. M. Melamed, Spinoza and Buddha:Visions of a Dead God (University of Chicago Press, 1933), p.324

similarities in their overall world view. Both Buddha and Jesus seemed to believe in a non-physical essence from which everything in the physical world emerged.

Modern science might use the term "universal consciousness". Buddha referred to it as nirvana. Jesus referred to it as "Spirit" or "the Kingdom of God" or "the Kingdom of Heaven" or "Abba" (translated "Father" in the Bible), all of which suggest a broader and more nebulous concept of God.

Keep in mind that the modern Christian concept of "God" is not necessarily the concept Jesus had. Kabbalah, a type of Jewish mysticism, was common before and during the time of Jesus. Kabbalah has a less defined and more mystical concept of God than does traditional Judaism. Jesus' understanding of God seems similar.

Regardless of the language being used, the idea is that everything emerges from, and is a manifestation of, one non-physical essence. Buddha, along with modern psychology, suggested that our individual self is somewhat of an illusion. Jesus' teachings about dying to self, seeing ourselves in other people, and experiencing oneness with God and others seem to express a similar idea.

According to the Bible, Jesus taught that we are all ultimately connected like "branches on a vine" and that "the Kingdom of God is within". In other words, we all share a fundamental oneness with "Abba" and each other.

According to the Bible, on the night before he died, Jesus prayed that all people would experience "oneness" with each other and God (John 17). As an illustration of this "oneness", he also taught that when we help the stranger, the sick, the prisoner, etc., we are actually helping him (Matthew 25).

A rather striking example is in the gospel of John where, according to the Bible, Jesus claims, "I and the Father are one." The story continues, "Again his Jewish opponents picked up stones to stone him, but Jesus said to them, "I have shown you many good works from Abba. For which of these do you stone me?" "We are not stoning you for any good work," they replied, "but for blasphemy, because you, a mere man, claim to be God." Jesus answered them, "Is it not written in your Law, 'you all are God'? If your law called everyone 'God,'... Why then do you accuse me of blasphemy because I said, 'I am God's Son?'"

Here, Jesus seemed to justify his own claim of being one with God by quoting a Jewish scripture which claimed that all people are one with God. In other words, while traditional Christianity teaches that only Jesus is the incarnation of God, according to the Bible at least, Jesus seemed to teach that all human beings are "incarnations of God" or "manifestations of God" or "sons and daughters of God".

Sacraments

This original Buddhist idea of everything being just various manifestations of one thing was partially retained by the church in its doctrine of "sacraments". Catholic Christianity has always emphasized how God can be physically expressed in things, like water, bread and wine. The church calls these physical things "sacraments". According to the church, Jesus was the ultimate "sacrament".

But more in line with Buddhism, Jesus seemed to teach that everyone and everything is a "sacrament". "God" is fully present in and through everyone and everything, all the time.

Reincarnation

The Hindu and Buddhist idea of reincarnation can also express the idea of everything being the expression, manifestation or incarnation of one timeless essence. In this more liberal view of reincarnation, it's not just individual souls that keep reincarnating lifetime after lifetime; it's "God" (or whatever the word "God" points to) that keeps reincarnating over and over again as you, me and everything that exists. Again, this is basically taking the traditional Christian idea of Jesus being an incarnation of "God" and applying it to everyone and everything.

Most modern Christians don't realize that reincarnation was a common belief among Jews and early Christians. The Bible contains several examples. When Jesus asserted that John the Baptist was actually Elijah returning from the dead, this obviously suggested some type of reincarnation. When the disciples told Jesus that many saw him as "Jeremiah or one of the prophets returned from the dead", this also suggested reincarnation. In fact, the church did not officially declare reincarnation a heresy until 553 AD – over 500 years after the time of Jesus.

Eternal Life

The idea that everything is ultimately one thing allowed both Buddha and Jesus to challenge the universal fear of death. Most of us only identify with what psychologists call our "ego", which gives us the sense of being a separate individual self. Buddha and Jesus both seemed to teach that this small, separate "self" is either an illusion or at least temporary and insignificant. Ultimately, we are all manifestations of one larger "self", which never dies.

According to the Bible, Jesus seems to have taught that when we begin to identify with this larger eternal self, rather than with our smaller individual self, we "pass from death into life". We immediately begin to experience "eternal life". Buddha would say the veils of Maya fall away and we become "enlightened".

According to the Bible Jesus said, "Unless a grain of wheat falls to the earth and dies, it remains just a seed; but if it dies, it bears much fruit…If you love your life, you will lose it. But if you let it go, you will have it forever…Those who believe as me will never die." All these Biblical sayings of Jesus seem to point to a larger eternal self that we are all individual manifestations of.

Earthly Relationships

The idea of us all being manifestations of one "large eternal self" raises several questions regarding our current "small self". What happens to our "small self" at death? Are we like waves, which exist for a while, but then merge back into the ocean from which they came, to be remembered no more?

Buddha would probably answer yes and tell us to be more detached from earthly passions for that reason. Jesus may have been slightly more open to individual survival of death, but, according to the Bible, he certainly did not emphasize individual immortality the way modern Christianity does.

In the Bible, Jesus clearly taught detachment from earthly concerns, even making statements regarding family relationships that are harsh and difficult for westerners to understand. According to the Bible, Jesus told a potential disciple who wanted to bury his father, "Let the dead bury their own dead" (Luke 9:60).

According to the Bible, Jesus said, "If anyone comes to Me, and does not hate his own father and mother and wife and children and brothers and sisters, yes, and even his own life, he cannot be my disciple" (Luke 14:26). When his own mother and brothers came to see him, Jesus said, "Who are my mother and my brothers?" He then looked around and said, "Here are my mother and my brothers! Whoever does the will of God is my brother and sister and mother" (Mark 3:31–35).

Again, we don't know for sure if Jesus actually made such statements, but if he did, they obviously reflect the Buddhist idea that our small, earthly self is temporary and of far less importance than most assume.

I'll say more about it in the chapter on death, but, for now, let me emphasize this. Seeing our current individuality as a temporary manifestation of one eternal essence does not make our current individuality less meaningful. The fact that much of what we experience today may be forgotten over the years does not make today any less significant. The fact that memories of loved ones may fade over time, does not, in any way, make our loved ones less significant now. Again, there's much more to explore regarding what happens to individuals at death, and I will do so in a later section.

Love & Compassion

Finally, Buddha and Jesus also recognized that if everything is ultimately the manifold expression of just one thing, love and compassion for everything naturally follows. Knowing we are all various expressions of one thing helps us, not only fear death less, but also love each other more. Buddha and Jesus believed that, in a very real sense, we are all different versions of each other. It obviously follows that we should be kind to all these other versions of ourselves. As Buddha would say, "You are that".

The deep oneness and connectedness we all share suggests that the suffering of any of us affects all of us. Based on this, Buddha and Jesus taught that we should "bear one another's burdens", "forgive one another", "share with one another" and "treat others the way we want to be treated". We all do better when we all do better.

In conclusion, the similarities between Jesus and Buddha are striking and deep. As James M. Hanson of the University of Srinagar observes, "Was Jesus really a Buddhist? The answer is not yes or no, but rather to what extent Jesus was or was not a Buddhist."

The Perennial Philosophy

It seems likely that Jesus taught the same ideas of universal oneness and compassion that can be found in the mystical versions of almost every religion. Many call it the "perennial philosophy". It suggests that we are all expressions or manifestations of one eternal mystery.

Different writers have described it in different ways. In their book, *Journey of the Universe,* philosopher Brian Swimme and historian Mary Evelyn Tucker write, "For just as the Milky Way is the universe in the form of a galaxy, and an orchid is the universe in the form of a flower, we are the universe in the form of a human. And every time we are drawn to look up into the night sky and reflect on the awesome beauty of the universe, we are actually the universe reflecting on itself."

Sufism, a mystical form of Islam, has a famous saying, "You are the mirror in which God sees himself." The perennial philosophy sees God in everything, including those we often judge to be inferior or unworthy: so-called sinners and heretics, women, LGBTQ individuals, people from other races and ethnicities, the poor, those with disabilities, animals, non-Christians, and the Earth itself. Whether we're talking about Adam and Eve or chimpanzees, we all come from the same stock. We all breathe the same air and drink the same water. We all bleed the same blood. We are all one. We all belong.

Whether we use the term "God", "Nirvana", "Tao" or "Universal Consciousness", the message is the same. We all come from one essence and we all return to that one essence at death. The story of Jesus' birth, death and resurrection - regardless of whether one interprets it literally or metaphorically – reminds us of this cycle of birth, loss and renewal that characterizes everything in our universe.

Although it's seldom emphasized in modern evangelical Christianity, remnants of this perennial philosophy can still be found in many early Christian writings. In describing the goal of the Christian life, some of the earliest church leaders used the term "theosis", which literally means to become one with God. The Apostle Paul seems to describe a similar idea in his 1st letter to the church at Corinth, when he wrote that the ultimate destiny of all creation is "God becoming all in all" (1 Corinthians 15:28).

The perennial philosophy is also reflected in an early Christian hymn, quoted in Philippians 2:6 of the Bible, which describes an "emptying" that takes place when "God" becomes human. It says of Jesus, "Although he existed in the form of God...he emptied himself..." This "emptying" temporarily limited his knowledge and experience of being God. Thus the Bible has Jesus asking God from the cross, "Why have you forsaken me?" Jesus dies, but is then raised from the dead. He returns to "the right hand of God", and knows once again his prior and eternal existence as God. While the church limits this experience to Jesus, the original idea surely included us all.

Regardless of whether one takes the story literally or not, it reflects the perennial philosophy of one eternal source "emptying" itself to take on physical life, but then "returning" at death to full awareness of its eternal nature. According to the timeless teachings of Buddha, Jesus and many others, we are all on that journey back home from the limits of individual physical existence to the full freedom of our eternal oneness. Waking up to this truth is what Buddha called "enlightenment" and Jesus called entering or finding the "Kingdom of God" or the "Kingdom of Heaven".

Setting Jesus Free from Christianity

Whatever else Jesus or Buddha had in mind, most religious scholars are convinced that neither intended to start a new religion. Most believe they wanted to help people find freedom from religion - and, more specifically, the exploitation, hatred and fear that religion engenders. The universe was their temple, nature was their scripture, the seasons were their liturgy, and all human beings were their brothers and sisters.

According to the Gospel of Thomas, (one of the earliest gospels, but omitted from the Bible) Jesus said, "The Kingdom of God is inside you and all around you. Not in a mansion of wood and stone. Split a piece of wood and I am there. Lift a stone and you will find me."

Recognizing the similarities between Buddha and Jesus does not make Jesus less than what the church claims him to be. It makes him more (and it makes us more). Like Buddha, Jesus was an "enlightened" human being who wanted to share his revolutionary and transforming understanding of reality with others. And he knew it would always be bigger than any religion.

Like Buddha, Jesus never wanted to be worshiped. In fact Buddha said, "If you meet the Buddha, kill him." In other words don't focus on some ancient Buddha, become a "Buddha" yourself. I hear a similar message in Jesus' words from the Bible, "You will do greater things than me" and "It is enough for the student to be like the teacher." Buddha and Jesus simply wanted everyone to realize that we are all one, and then live accordingly.

So, listen with your heart. Which message rings true?

Jesus #1: You are a sinner and deserve hell. I died for your sins - God punished me in your place. If you will accept me and become part of the church, you will go to heaven. If you reject me, you will spend eternity in hell.

Jesus #2: Follow my example. Open your eyes to the oneness of everything. Share what you have with those in need. Enjoy life, but don't be selfish, and don't judge. We are all manifestations of God, so don't be afraid of death.

When you look at all the evidence and listen to your own heart, it should be obvious. Jesus was never about reward and punishment. Jesus was never about judging and condemning. Jesus was never about power and money. Jesus was about joy, freedom, compassion, forgiveness and hope.

Jesus hung out with "sinners" and outcasts, because they seemed to understand where he was coming from – more so than the "righteous" and the rich. He called out the rich, because they were exploiting the poor. He called out the "righteous", because they thought they were better than everyone else. But he offered everyone the same freedom and forgiveness, if they would simply open their eyes.

I'm reminded of another saying of Jesus from Matthew 6:22-23, "The eye is the lamp of the body. If your eyes are healthy, your whole body will be full of light. But if your eyes are unhealthy, your whole body will be full of darkness."

The church's Jesus often becomes little more than a good luck charm or a magic wand. If you say the right words and believe the right things, then Jesus will protect you from the devil and give you a free pass to heaven. (He may even help you find a parking place at the grocery store.)

The church's Jesus is just another religious fairy tale used to divide us. Our side is right; their side is wrong. You must choose sides. Bullshit! For the sake of human destiny, we need to wake up and realize we're all on the same side, whether we want to be or not.

Along with naïve and dangerous views of the Bible, as well as concepts of "sin" that judge and condemn, Christianity's version of Jesus is just another example of dishonest religious exploitation. It's time to see the truth and be free.

The Value of Religion

In spite of all the deception and disunity that marks most religion; it obviously contains value for some. I personally know many people who have found peace, hope and healing through religion. Millions who have lost loved ones have found comfort in the church and the church's message. Thousands of addicts have found freedom in the church. The church has served as an emotional and spiritual hospital for many.

But millions more find the same peace and healing outside of religion. The dynamics that allow churches to provide hope and healing, have less to do with religion and more to do with the relationships religion provides. Religion, in most cases, simply provides the context.

Secondly, religious groups often help the poor. There are numerous examples of religious groups standing up against social and economic injustice. Catholic Charities and the Salvation Army are to be applauded for the work they do on behalf of the poor and powerless, both in the US and around the world.

Still, governments and non-religious organizations do far more. Sadly, only a small percentage of religious money finds its way outside the religion. The vast majority of religious wealth remains inside the institution and is used to pay the enormous expenses required to maintain the system.

My experience with both small and large churches in both Protestant and Catholic traditions makes me very skeptical that religious charities could ever replace tax payer supported safety nets like Food Stamps, Disaster Relief, Medicaid, Medicare, Social Security, public education, etc.

Thirdly, religion – at least the mystical approaches to religion – often encourages people to develop a more intuitive approach to knowing truth. Contemplative prayer and meditation are examples. In many ways, life is what Zen Buddhism calls a koan. A koan is basically a riddle that forces us to a place where reason and intellect no longer provide answers – forcing us to trust a deeper intuition, a deeper way of knowing.

You can spend the rest of your life reading what a rose smells like, but you will never understand fully until you smell a rose. You can spend the rest of your life studying particular ideas, but some ideas can never be fully appreciated until you experience them directly. Until then they are mostly reflections of something that cannot be fully expressed in words.

For centuries, people looked at the moon and thought they were seeing a true light. Ultimately, they realized the moon had no light of its own, but was simply reflecting a tiny bit of light from the sun. In a similar way, our words and ideas, at best, only reflect a tiny bit of the infinite mystery behind existence - a mystery that, to some degree, at least for now, can only be known intuitively. To the degree that religion helps you develop and trust your own sense of intuitive knowing, it may have value.

Unfortunately, most religions limit your ability to trust authorities outside of their particular religion, whether it's science, your own experience or your own intuition. This contradicts Jesus, who, according to the Bible, said, "the spirit (not a book or an institution) will guide you to all truth." Both Biblical and non-Biblical documents quote Jesus as saying, "The Kingdom of God is within you." But, again most religion is threatened by such personal freedom to seek truth however and wherever it may be found.

Finally, part of religion's value lies in the stories it tells. We all need stories to help us make sense of life. It's helpful to step back occasionally and see your own life as a story. A life with no underlying story or sense of purpose is like disconnected, repetitive, and meaningless dreams.

But, again, some of the most valuable stories humans need to hear come from outside religion. Most religious stories have non-religious versions. I've found that Hollywood often does a far better job telling important stories than religion does.

So the question is this. Is all the division and dishonesty that characterizes religion worth the benefit it sometimes provides? While religion may benefit millions of people, there seems to be far better ways to receive those same benefits, without the dishonest and divisive exploitation religion embodies. That brings us to science.

Science

"The religion of the future will be a cosmic religion. It should transcend personal God and avoid dogma and theology. Covering both the natural and the spiritual, it should be based on a religious sense arising from the experience of all things natural and spiritual as a meaningful unity,"
Albert Einstein

"Therefore every scribe who has been trained for the kingdom of heaven is like a master of a house, who brings out of his treasure what is new and what is old," Jesus

When we ask the "big questions" and think about ultimate reality, we will always over simplify. We can't help it. We have to speculate and guess. We know so little – far, far less than we think. Our attempts to understand ultimate reality are like an ant trying to understand quantum physics. So we must stay humble. We must always end our statements regarding the "big questions" with, "Maybe, maybe not. I wonder"[6].

Still, having said that, we do know a lot. We know far more than we used to know, and we know enough to offer speculations that are valuable.

Both religion and science seek truth. The difference between religion and science, however, is that while science allows itself to evolve and continue learning new truth, religion does not. Religion, too often, refuses to let go of ideas long disproven and no longer relevant.

Science may do this too for a little while, because scientists have egos, and they, too, often find it painful to let go of ideas they've invested a

---

[6] Embracing Uncertainty: Breakthrough Methods for Achieving Peace of Mind When Facing the Unknown,
Susan Jeffers, 2004

lifetime in. But they do, ultimately, because that is the nature of science. Unlike religion, science expects old beliefs to be replaced by new ones. It welcomes the new discoveries that disprove old theories.

In contrast, religion often claims to possess absolute and final truth. It institutionalizes those absolutes and invests immoral amounts of money and energy in defending them. It usually claims some type of divine authority. Obviously it loses credibility when "divine authority" is proven wrong. A major weakness of conservative Christianity is that it tends to resist science. Such blindness and arrogance is foolish and dangerous.

Liberal religion tries to maintain historical and scientific credibility. It tries to take history, psychology, physics and neuroscience seriously and allow itself to evolve accordingly. Obviously, not all approaches to religion are equally bad.

Still, science is ultimately the better approach to truth. Human society will be far better off when the scientific method replaces religion as our ultimate standard of authority. Catholic priest, Thomas Berry, suggests that we are now living in between the story that religion tells and the story that science tells. Whatever is true within religion and spirituality, will ultimately be discovered by science. The story of our universe will then be more complete than ever before.

So, as I close out this rather long section, I repeat my main point. Religion, more times than not, becomes an obstacle to discovering truth. Humans need freedom from religion and the exploitation it almost always engenders. A free approach based on objective science is the better way.

A Hopeful Trend

My son once asked me, "Dad, with so many preachers teaching so many different things, how can we know what to believe?" Perhaps this partly explains why so many young people are leaving religion. Perhaps that's not a bad thing.

A 2012 poll released by WIN-Gallup International suggests that all religion is on the decline worldwide, and especially in America where Christianity dominates. The poll - using interviews with more than 50,000 people in 57 countries representing 73% of the world's population - asked participants, "irrespective of whether they attended a place of worship, if they considered themselves to be religious, not religious, or an atheist."

The resulting data showed the number of people worldwide who call themselves religious is now 59 %, compared to 68 % in 2005. Currently 13 % percent identify themselves as atheist, compared to 4 % in 2005.

Ireland, the U.S., France and Canada were among the top 10 countries which have experienced a "notable decline in religiosity" since 2005. The number of people in the U.S. who claim to be religious dropped from 73 % to 60 %. In addition, 5 % of Americans identified themselves as atheists, compared to 1 % in 2005.

As someone who spent decades in the Christian ministry, studying the Bible, praying, helping people, and, yes, judging people as well, I now believe this is a good trend.

Below are verses I wrote a few years ago, trying to express in a more poetic way, the journey that I, along with many others, have taken from evangelical, "Bible believing" religion to a much more honest and joyful state of intellectual and spiritual freedom.

Evolution

It has to be this or that.
Paradoxes are not allowed,
They must be resolved.
If one wins,
Another must lose.
Dualism reigns.
"The Bible tells me so".

But then:
A child divorces.
A family member is gay.
Trajedy strikes.
Life is more complicated than I thought.
A co-worker is Muslim
Or agnostic or atheist,
They act more like Jesus
Than "we" do.

A "good" Samaritan?
A "faithful" Syro-Phoenician woman?
A "godly" sinner?

My righteousness
Is only fear
Parading as righteousness.
All those not like me,
Are just like me.
I am one of "them".
Or even less!
My judgments return like a boomerang -
And strike a fatal wound.

My safe and familiar world
Falls apart.
Confusion reigns.
The pieces no longer fit.

I'm lost.
It feels like death.
"My God, my God!
Why hast thou forsaken me?"

I deny.
I bargain.
I become angry
I weep.
I let go.
"Into thy hands I commit my spirit."

God becomes a Mystery.
Truth becomes a journey.
Love casts out fear.
Everything belongs.
It all just is.
It's all good.

But the chosen remain frozen,
While sinners and heretics
Enter the Kingdom of God.

Freedom from Political & Economic Exploitation

"Politics is the art of looking for trouble, finding it everywhere, diagnosing it incorrectly and applying the wrong remedies," Groucho Marx

I've already noted how easy it is for political groups to exploit religion. The Roman Emperor, Constantine, hi-jacked Christianity 1700 years ago for political exploitation. It continues to this day, one example being the exploitation of conservative Christianity by the Republican Party in the United States during the latter part of the 20th century. But while religion is an often used tool, political exploitation is primarily about money and power. Economic and political exploitation is the second major "demon" we need to be set free from.

At its most fundamental level, politics is a struggle for power. Most commonly, it ends up being a wrestling match between the most powerful and the least powerful, the rich and the poor, the "haves" and the "have nots", the business owners and the workers. This struggle has taken various forms over the centuries, but the players are always the same: those who use their good fortune to exploit and those of lesser fortune who get exploited.

The winners always write the history books. As a result, the ideologies of the rich and powerful tend to have the most lasting influence on culture. Sadly, our religion, our economic system and our politics almost always reflects the world views of wealthy and powerful political winners; not less wealthy and less powerful political losers.

In most cases, those who challenge the "powers that be" are defeated quickly and easily. Once power is established, it's much easier to maintain power than to challenge it. Still, there are those rare, yet historically significant, times when the masses are desperate for change and strong leaders rise up who can organize the masses and bring about change.

Often, a strong but selfish leader will exploit the situation and make things worse, possibly moving toward some type of dictatorship. But occasionally a wise and compassionate leader will be available to rescue the masses and move them toward freedom and greater well being.

History reveals several examples of less powerful groups successfully challenging the more powerful status quo. The growth of unions and other successful labor movements during the early 20th century is one. The modern civil rights movement in the United States under Martin Luther King, Jr. is another. India's non-violent struggle for independence under Mahatma Gandhi, the American and French Revolutions, the Protestant Reformation, numerous other reforms triggered by the teachings and martyrdom of Jesus, as well as the Jewish exodus from Egyptian slavery under Moses are all examples of large powerless groups escaping exploitation from smaller but more powerful elites.

Two important points follow. First and sadly, major struggles for freedom are often marked by bloodshed and martyrdom. Violent revolution is the norm. It's encouraging, however, that Martin Luther King, Jr. and Mahatma Gandhi, inspired by the teachings of both Buddha and Jesus, led revolutions that were predominantly non-violent.

Secondly, and even more sadly, over time those who gain freedom fail to maintain it. Greedy forces will arise from within the new group, allowing a smaller elite group to once again take control. At some point, the new leaders begin to believe and act just like the old leaders that once exploited them. At first, the new leaders may not recognize what is occurring. Later they either live in denial or find clever ways to justify their new cycle of exploitation.

A clear example is Protestant Christianity, which has become just as dishonest and divisive as the older Catholic religion it once revolted against. Just like their Catholic forefathers, institutional survival gradually became their main priority, fueling the need for more money and more favor with the upper class – at the expense of honesty and freedom.

New and promising political parties follow the same unfortunate pattern. It was this keen understanding of how greed operates in every society that led Thomas Jefferson to suggest the need for a social revolution every few generations. This cycle from exploitation to revolution to freedom but then back to exploitation seems to repeat itself again and again in every society. To understand why, follow the money.

Two Economic Worldviews

Politics always comes down to economics, and the pendulum of economic power is always swinging in one of two directions. Moving in one direction will be those committed to "survival of the fittest". They insist that "only the strong survive". In their worldview, it's important to always "look out for number one". "Might makes right" is their deeply held belief. "Every man for himself" is their creed.

Moving in the opposite direction will be those committed to a "no one left behind" strategy". They are convinced that "united we stand – divided we fall". History has taught this group that "we all do better when we all do better". "All for one and one for all" is their mantra", and "compassion for the poor and weak" is their prime directive.

Actually, both approaches have their strengths and weaknesses. Both also risk being taken to unhealthy extremes. The "no one left behind" approach can sometimes lose focus on individual responsibility, while the "survival of the fittest" approach often results in exploitative monopolies, oligarchies and plutocracies. Wealthy elites will always favor "survival of the fittest".

Is there any way to manage this economic roller coaster? Is it possible to limit extremes and maintain some degree of socio-economic balance? Can an extreme and unhealthy gap between the rich and the poor be avoided? Even more challenging, can the natural human greed that drives such disparity be offset by less destructive virtues?

Those with wealth and power will argue that allowing them to pursue individual success, without being weighted down by concerns for the rest of society, is actually the better long term approach. They claim it will achieve innovations and breakthroughs that, while hurting the weak in the short term, help everyone in the long term. They insist that it ultimately creates a rising tide which raises all ships. In other words, "we all do better when we allow a few to do a whole lot better".

Other phrases like "trickle down" "job creation", "deregulation", "tax cuts" and "wasteful government spending" will find its way into most of their talking points. Unfortunately, while there is some truth to their claims, they ignore other socio-economic factors that are just as important, if not more so.

Those opposing a "survival of the fittest" approach will argue that forcing the strong to help the weak along the way, while it may penalize the strong in the short term, will open the possibility for even greater innovations and breakthroughs for everyone in the long term. A poor immigrant child, for example, might be given an educational opportunity resulting in some world changing discovery, that would otherwise be missed. Some of the weak who would be left behind in the first option would be given more educational and economic opportunities in the second option, which would allow for historical breakthroughs not seen in the first option. In other words, "we all do better when we all do better", both in the short term and the long term.

This group will also argue that "showing compassion for the poor and weak" and "leaving no one behind" is simply the right thing to do. They insist that "it's not all about money". Not everyone agrees with this position, but many do. Renowned sages like Moses, Buddha, Confucius and Jesus consistently emphasize compassion and mercy, while denouncing greed and selfishness. Those who value their social teachings would normally lean toward the "no one left behind" approach as opposed to "survival of the fittest".

Interestingly, most do not know that, according to the Bible, Jesus said more about money than any other one topic - and virtually all of it was bad. Some of Jesus' most damning statements were made toward the rich. Avoiding greed and showing immediate compassion toward the poor - both individually and as a society - seems to be at the heart of what Buddha and Jesus taught.

Lessons from the Past

"If you are rich, you have to be an idiot not to stay rich. And if you are poor, you have to be really smart to get rich,"
John Green

A key requirement for finding and maintaining freedom is the ability to learn from the past. As philosopher, George Santayana warned over 100 years ago, "Those who cannot remember the past are condemned to repeat it"[7]. History has a lot to teach us regarding politics and economics. It clearly shows how a "survival of the fittest" approach easily dominates over time, and almost always leads to significant income disparity and social inequality; which in turn usually results in political and economic exploitation.

Just like in the classic game of Monopoly, the playing field quickly becomes uneven allowing economic inequality to slowly but surely increase. By the way, the game of Monopoly was invented in the early 20th century to illustrate this fact.

It's undeniable and unavoidable that some individuals will always be given an economic advantage due to birth, family resources, cultural norms and random events. You cannot over state the value of "knowing the right person" or "being in the right place at the right time".

Nor can you over state the disadvantages of "not knowing the right people" or "being in the wrong place at the wrong time". Some individuals will naturally gain more wealth over time, as others lose wealth over time, due to the above random factors.

Ultimately, a few will amass excessive wealth, leading to excessive

---

[7] The Life of Reason: Reason in Common Sense. Scribner's, 1905: 284

power and political influence. As a result, a wealthy minority will gradually gain control of most private and public enterprises, including local, state and federal governments.

Sadly, few are ever content with what they have. Greed creates a thirst for more, even if they have to take it from those who have much less. Overtime, social safety nets and other assistance programs designed to help make up for what was not given to the less fortunate at birth or during childhood, will be attacked by the wealthy. These life lines to the poor will be labeled as wasteful entitlements that do more harm than good.

Ultimately, high rates of poverty, high rates of crime, poor health outcomes, less educational opportunities, broad discrimination, a shrinking middle class, fear mongering and other political propaganda will become the norm. As the disparity between a wealthy "few" and a poor "many" increases, society will become less stable.

Acts of violence will increase along with other symptoms of a declining society. Ultimately, the plight of the poor masses will become desperate, while wealthy elites become even more arrogant and blind. When warned that the poor have no bread, their reply will be "let them eat cake".

At that point, some type of revolution is unavoidable to restore balance. Then the cycle starts all over again. Any student of history will recognize this pattern playing out again and again across the centuries.

Interestingly, as I write these words in December of 2017, the top 1% of the US population owns 40% of the wealth. The bottom 90% owns 27% of the wealth. While most developed countries offset wealth inequality by allowing tax dollars to pay for everyone's healthcare, education and childcare, the US does not.

The US relies more heavily on free market capitalism than most other developed countries. While this approach obviously favors the wealthy, they claim it ultimately benefits everyone. Our Republican dominated U.S. Congress just passed a major tax bill that will give major, permanent tax cuts to the wealthy; and small, temporary tax cuts to everyone else. Again, they are claiming it will boost the economy and ultimately benefit everyone. Personally, I have my doubts, but time will tell.

We Believe What We Want to Believe

Obviously, avoiding the natural progression toward socio-economic inequality and exploitation would be a wonderful accomplishment. It would avoid a lot of social injustice and make the world a better place. But is it possible?

The Jewish Bible (Christian Old Testament) describes Israel's ancient attempt to resist this natural progression toward economic exploitation by establishing a "Year of Jubilee." Every 70 years, all the land in Israel was to be returned to the original families and all debts were to be canceled. The idea was to periodically restore a level economic playing field. Not surprisingly, the "powers that be" never fully implemented the plan.

1000 years later, the first followers of Jesus also tried to resist this natural flow toward socio-economic inequality by doing away with all personal property. According to the Christian New Testament, the first Jewish followers of Jesus gave up ownership of their property and began to share everything. Like the "Year of Jubilee" this attempt to erase the disparity between the rich and poor also failed.

It failed partly due to Jewish and Roman persecution of the new movement. The "powers that be" had already crucified Jesus. This movement, based on Jesus' teachings, was obviously seen as a continuing threat. It ultimately failed because of the nature and power of human greed.

For multiple reasons, it's extremely hard for us humans to give up what we have attained. Our natural survival instincts cause us to be naturally selfish and greedy. Our egos need to be stroked and admired. Change is always risky and uncomfortable.

When destiny and lady luck smile on a few of us, it's difficult to share our good fortune with those beyond our particular family and tribe. As Americans, our unique history of rugged individualism enforces these natural tendencies.

A few may share some of their good fortune with others, but very few are willing to change the system that favored them so lucratively. It's easier to convince ourselves that our good fortune was actually hard work, and the bad fortune of everyone else was the result of laziness and bad choices.

The fortunate ones, even though they were actually "born on third base", find it easy to start believing they "hit a triple". In their minds, they worked hard and made good choices. The poor did not; else they would be wealthy, too.

This naïve and convenient narrative can easily be challenged, but for a long time, even the poor masses may buy into its logic. It will sound reasonable, as long as they don't hear the other side and life doesn't become intolerable. They may be content with simply having a job and be thankful to the rich "boss man" for providing it.

Many will give up seeking a better life here and place their hope in some heavenly afterlife. Wealthy religious people will often see their good fortune as a blessing from God, and who are they to question God? Most of us believe what we want to believe, so it's easy to justify economic inequality and exploitation.

"Liberal"

How do you free yourself from political and economic exploitation? At the risk of over simplifying, which is always dangerous and in need of further clarification - which I will do - let me just say this. To be free, you must question modern conservative talking points that protect those in power, and listen carefully to the more liberal ideas that have set people free throughout history.

The word "liberal" is a nasty word for many people, especially in the south and many rural area of the United States. That's unfortunate because the word "liberal", which basically means free and generous, has historically been used to describe those who try to help society avoid the political and economic exploitation described above. It's always the rich and powerful who trash liberals the most.

When Thomas Jefferson penned the Declaration of Independence, he was driven by liberal ideas such as liberty, freedom and equality - elevating basic human rights above the rights of kings, dictators and wealthy elites.

Our United States Constitution established structures to guarantee these rights, along with a mechanism to make amendments when necessary. Without these amendments, our constitution would become a dead document, easily exploited by the rich and powerful.

Moving forward almost 100 years, a very progressive and liberal thinking Abraham Lincoln dared to challenge wealthy, southern plantation owners by ending slavery. He was followed by other liberals who challenged unjust systems which oppressed women, the working poor and minorities.

As you walk through history, it becomes clear that most human progress is driven by liberal ideas and liberal people. Monopolies, plutocracies and oligarchies always demand liberal challenges.

In spite of how passionately conservative Christians will deny it, Jesus was obviously very liberal and progressive by the standards of his day (and ours). Jesus challenged systems that allowed the powerful and wealthy to oppress and exploit the poor, the foreigner, and others who were not part of the status quo.

And as is often the case, the system labeled him a dangerous enemy, spread fear and anger among the masses, and finally killed him. Other famous liberals like Lincoln, Gandhi, Kennedy and King met similar fates.

The Jewish prophets of old were extremely liberal in their speaking out against exploitative Jewish kings and priests. Not surprisingly, the "powers that be" accused them of being dangerous and unpatriotic liberals.

Liberal movements tend to promote peace, justice and diplomacy while conservative movements tend to promote fear, distrust and aggressive first strikes. Liberal movements give hope to the poor and weak, while conservative movements tend to protect their more affluent peers with large police forces and strong militaries.

Liberal eyes tend to see the bigger picture and think globally, while conservative eyes tend to focus on a smaller world comprised of people like them. Liberals minds value diversity and are open to learning new things. Conservatives minds prefer uniformity and traditional thinking in both religion and politics.

Liberal ideology stands up for human rights, builds hospitals, supports labor laws, and establishes social safety nets like Social Security, Medicare and Medicaid. Conservative ideology often wants to dismantle these hard earned liberal victories and return to a more primitive and painful past.
Liberals support free market capitalism – it was originally a liberal concept. But liberals would never promote capitalism as the answer to everything. Conservatives might.

Even the God set forth by Jesus is an undeniable liberal. Jesus' God is creative, generous, liberating and forgiving, always standing up for the poor and the weak, against the wealthy and powerful. This is the basis for the Catholic doctrine which gives "preferential treatment to the poor". It's why any credible Protestant Bible scholar will admit that the God of the Bible is always on the side of the poor. According to the Bible, when Mary, Jesus' mother, realized God was giving her a son, she began to sing, "He has filled the hungry with good things, and the rich he has sent away empty."

Liberal ideas, both religious and political, have always been the best defense against economic and political exploitation. Liberals know that "we all do better when we all do better." In order to attain and maintain freedom from political and economic exploitation, liberal approaches to government must be defended and promoted.

First, let's be clear that liberals are not communists. Second, liberals may see value is some elements of socialism, but they are not socialists in the way most conservatives portray them. The democratic socialism promoted by some liberals is simply an approach to democracy that protects society from exploitation at the hands of small but powerful wealthy elites.

Labels are misleading and dangerous. I hesitate even using them, but they have historical and technical value, when used honestly and accurately. In that context, I whole heartedly stand by the following statement. In order to be free from the exploitation described in these pages – religious, economic and political – you must become more liberal and progressive in your thinking.

You must be willing to think outside small, outdated conservative boxes. You must not be afraid of new ideas or new people who look and act differently than you. You must choose to go forward not backward. The so called "glorious past" that so many conservatives want you to return to, is not so glorious. The changing times that so many conservatives fear, are hopeful times, full of potential and freedom.

You must separate yourself from conservative voices that condemn other groups based on religion, nationality, lifestyle, gender and age. Live and let live. There's plenty of room on this planet, and in your town, for people with different beliefs and backgrounds.

Be willing to challenge the false patriotism promoted by conservatives that refuses to admit America's failures. Be willing to learn from other nations and cultures.

Finally, reject the extreme individualism that disregards the common good. One example is gun rights. Yes, you have a constitutional right to purchase guns, but when easy access to assault rifles and large magazines are used again and again to kill large numbers of young people, it's time to consider the common good and implement common sense limits.

Young people also have a right to "life, liberty and the pursuit of happiness." People kill people but they kill many more people when they have easy access to military rifles designed to kill many people rapidly. Again, don't just focus on individual rights and neglect the rights of society as a whole.

Do all of the above, not just with your belief, but with your behavior. Not just with your voice, but with your vote. Our United States government is not something in Washington DC that you have no control over. You are part of the government and it ultimately reflects the priorities of you and your fellow citizens.

Don't let the opinions of a bunch of old while people like me have the final word. Vote in every election and encourage your friends to do the same.

Victim's Top 6 List

While many controversial social issues are complicated and proponents on both sides can make valid arguments, others are more easily seen for what they are – exploitation. Here is my top 6 list of political and economic exploitations that demand immediate intervention on behalf of the victims. A thorough study is beyond the scope of this book, but I will briefly comment on each one.

Imprisonment – The United States locks up a higher percentage of its population than any other country. China is a distant second. Far too much of our love affair with prisons is driven by those who reap huge financial benefits from the current system.

Private prisons and government contracts related to private, state and federal prisons are extremely lucrative. There are much cheaper and healthier ways to treat those who break our laws. Some of our laws need changing.

Education – Attaining a quality education in the United States is becoming far too expensive, especially at the college and graduate level. Public education does not receive enough public funding to adequately prepare our young people for the future. We seem to be forgetting how dependent all societies are on a well educated populace.

Historically, only powerful elites who need the masses to be uneducated, so they can stay in power, favor weakening or privatizing public education. Unlike most other developed nations, we are quickly moving in that direction.

We also need to re-think the way we do education. It's important to teach our children, not what to think, but how to think. Our approach to education should integrate the hands, the head and the heart – the whole child – not just one dimension of their development.

It's important to recognize that most children do not fit into traditional educational frameworks. The best learning happens when students are free to move, explore, create, express and reason at their own pace. Hearing and interacting with stories, for example, is more effective than just memorizing facts.

Oligarchy (Government by the Wealthy) – Our entire political system is far too dependent on money. It seems that only the wealthy can afford to run for most state and federal offices. Even then, they depend on wealthy donors and lobbyists to be competitive and remain in office. Genuine campaign finance reform and reasonable term limits are items we desperately need to discuss as a society.

Healthcare – The United States spends far more per capita on healthcare than any other nation. Yet we have some of the worst outcomes. In areas where our system does well, the average citizen has very limited access to it due to how expensive it is.

Due to the lobbying power of pharmaceuticals and insurance companies, we are the only developed nation that does not have a "Medicare for all" approach. Big Pharma and Big Insurance own too many of our politicians on both sides of the aisle. Once again, it comes down to money, and far too many people are getting rich on those of us who are sick or old.

Our healthcare system focuses on treating illnesses rather than preventing or curing them, primarily because that's where the money is. We need to think outside the box and be open to new approaches to healthcare. We can learn from other countries and other approaches within our own country. Again, do the research and be smart.

Social Security and Medicare – Too many young people have accepted the wealthy elite's propaganda that Social Security and Medicare won't be around when they need it. They will be, and they will be stronger than ever if we vote for people who will protect and strengthen them.

The truth is not that we can't afford such entitlements. The truth is we can't afford, as a society, not to have them. The problem is the wealthy don't need them and don't want to help pay for them.

They are counting on younger generations to not know how life was in the United States before Social Security and Medicare. Unfortunately, those who would remember are no longer with us. Young adults should do some research before it's too late.

Prejudice – Because of religion and plain old ignorance, too many groups in our society are seen as threatening and undesirable. It's natural to fear that which is different, but modern, well educated societies should not fall victim to such blindness.

Who benefits when our natural prejudices are stirred up? It's usually a politician who can't get elected any other way... or an employer who needs cheap labor... or a religious leader who needs an enemy to rail against. Live and let live. Be free and let others be free.

It's Complicated

One of the ways the wealthy "powers that be" keep exploiting the masses is by oversimplify issues and forcing people to only think in terms of "either/or" rather than "both/and". In other words, if you are a conservative Republican, you must be for all of this and against all of this. If you are a liberal Democrat, you must be for all of this and against all of this. The truth is that most of us are all over the map on particular issues. You may label me a "liberal" but I'm fairly conservative on several issues.

For example, I personally think abortion should be limited. I think there may be situations where the death penalty is the lesser of two evils. Regarding gun ownership, I support the 2nd amendment, but I also believe there should be common sense limits. Not every person should be able to own a gun. And some types of weapons should be strictly regulated.

In other words, there will always be exceptions to any law or any right.

There will always be gray areas where hard judgments and painful compromises are the only solution. Come on, that's just common sense. Any politician or preacher who argues otherwise is exploiting some of the emotional or cultural blind spots we all possess.

Be willing to question your own leaders and think outside the box. Be willing to question yourself and allow your own thinking to evolve. Unfortunately, ideal situations seldom present themselves in real life. More times than not, society must choose between the lesser of two evils.

Most of us want the same things in life for ourselves and our loved ones. We only disagree on what approach to take. Rather than demonize each other, we must give each other the benefit of the doubt. We must listen to each other, avoid extremes and be willing to compromise.

We must avoid simplistic thinking and what some call "argument by anecdote". In other words, both sides can always find several specific examples or personal anecdotes to support their position. Sharing particular stories back and forth can go on forever. At some point you have to look at the bigger picture and consider large amounts of data.

Even then, you have to look at data from both sides. There still may not be full agreement, but at least you have increased the chances of making a healthy compromise. If we remain open and honest, things will become clearer as time goes by, and improvements can continue to be made.

Of course, modern politicians, preachers and media seem hesitant to take this approach. It doesn't stir up the base, generate large financial gifts or make good sound bites. Extreme positions, stubborn attitudes and outrageous statements are more entertaining and lucrative. But we all suffer in the long run.

People Become Like Their God

"I'm completely in favor of the separation of Church and State. These two institutions screw us up enough on their own, so both of them together is certain death,"
George Carlin

The first two sections of this book are about religion and politics. Even though we try to separate the two, we really can't. The majority of humans are religious. Many are driven toward religion by suffering or a fear of death. Most people's religion is a result of cultural brainwashing from childhood. Some just want there to be a more to life than what they now experience, so they remain open and hopeful.

Regardless of its source, religion affects our politics. Conservative religion usually supports conservative political movements, just as liberal religion usually supports liberal political movements. Another way to say it is this. Your image of "God" (or lack thereof) will determine your political views, and ultimately make you more or less vulnerable to political exploitation.

The more you study the Bible with an open and honest spirit, the more obvious it becomes that there are two very different "Gods" being described within its pages. Furthermore, there are two very different groups of people being described. Both gradually become like the particular version of "God" they believe in.

First notice what I consider the more traditional, conservative version of "God". Not all, but large parts of the Biblical Old Testament reflect this version of God.

In the book of Ezekiel, God said, "Therefore I will act in wrath. My eye will not spare, nor will I have pity. And though they cry in my ears with a loud voice, I will not hear them. I will execute great vengeance on them with wrathful rebukes. Then they will know that I am the Lord, when I lay my vengeance upon them."

In the book of Malachi, God said, "I have loved Jacob, but Esau I have hated."

When the Israelites were about to enter the "promised land" of Canaan, according to the book of Deuteronomy, God said, "You must utterly destroy them. You shall make no covenant with them, and show no mercy to them. You shall destroy all the peoples that the LORD your God will give over to you, your eye shall not pity them. You shall save alive nothing that breathes, but you shall utterly destroy them".

Generations later, when Israel was threatened by another enemy, God said to King Saul, "Now go and strike Amalek and utterly destroy all that he has, and do not spare him; but put to death both man and woman, child and infant, ox and sheep, camel and donkey."

Regarding sex, according to the book of Leviticus, God said, "If a man lies with a male as with a woman, both of them have committed an abomination; they shall be put to death." God went on to say, "If a man commits adultery with another man's wife, the adulterer and the adulteress shall surely be put to death."

Here are a few other statements from the Bible that also reflect the more traditional Christian version of God:

Deut. 22:20 - But if this charge is true, that the girl was not found a virgin, then they shall bring out the girl to the doorway of her father's house, and the men of her city shall stone her to death."
Exodus 21:17 - And he that curses his father, or his mother, shall surely be put to death.
Leviticus 20:10 - And the man that commits adultery with another man's wife, even he that commits adultery with his neighbor's wife, the adulterer and the adulteress shall surely be put to death.
Leviticus 24:16 - And he that blasphemes the name of the LORD, he shall surely be put to death, and all the congregation shall certainly stone him.
Exodus 21:7 - If a man sells his daughter as a servant; she is not to go free as male servants do.
Exodus 35:2 - For six days, work is to be done, but the seventh day shall

be your holy day, a day of Sabbath rest to the LORD. Whoever does any work on it is to be put to death.

It should come as no surprise that the followers of this "God" have a similar worldview. In their minds, justice is not about blind and broken people who need to be healed; it's about bad and sinful and people who need to be punished. Therefore, in their minds, we need to build more prisons, lock up more people, apply the death penalty and preach about hell.

It's easy to understand why the followers of this God treated Native Americans so cruelly. It's easy to understand their attitudes toward the Japanese, Jews, Muslims, Mexicans, blacks and gays. Cries to deport, segregate, imprison and kill are easily justified. Efforts to secure our borders, strengthen our police, build up our military and bomb our enemies are to be expected.

Many followers of this God will argue that slavery and Jim Crow were not that bad. They will insist that certain types of sex between consenting adults is wrong and should be legislated.

Bottom line: the traditional, conservative "God" of the Bible judges, discriminates, excludes, hates, punishes, demands violence and condones the horrors of war. **And people become like their god.**

Now, consider the more liberal version of "God" that also appears in the Bible and the Old Testament. This is the "God" described in the teachings of Jesus, who, by the way, was persecuted and ultimately crucified for challenging the traditional, conservative version of "God".

In the book of Isaiah, God said, "You are precious in my sight. I love you. Do not fear; I am with you. There is no one who can take you out of my hand. I have loved you with an everlasting love. I take no pleasure in the death of the wicked. With everlasting loving kindness I will have compassion on you. I will not be angry with you nor will I reject you."

In Leviticus, God said, "The stranger who resides with you shall be to you as the native among you, and you shall love him as yourself, for you were aliens in the land of Egypt. Do not seek revenge or bear a grudge against one of your people, but love your neighbor as yourself."

Jesus quoted the above verse later and we now know it as the "golden rule".

The "liberal God" told King David, the successor of King Saul, "You are not to build a house for my Name, because you are a warrior and have shed blood."

Later in the Old Testament, we find these words. "The soul of the Lord hates those who love violence. Wisdom is better than weapons of war."

In the book of Isaiah we find, "They shall beat their swords into plowshares, and their spears into pruning hooks; nation shall not lift up sword against nation, neither shall they learn war anymore."

In the New Testament, we find many reflections of this more liberal God. John writes, "God is love. Nothing can separate us from the love of God. Those who love, know God; those who do not love, do not know God." Paul writes, "It is not God's will that any should perish. God will reconcile all things to himself."

Jesus obviously recognized the two different versions of God in the Old Testament, and chose the more liberal version. He said, "Treat others the way you want to be treated. Love your enemies and pray for those who persecute you. If someone strikes you on the right cheek, offer them the other cheek. Those who live by the sword will die by the sword."

When a group of men were about to stone a woman caught in adultery (As the traditional version of God had commanded), Jesus said, "let him that is without sin cast the first stone."

As noted earlier, Jesus, himself, never condemned homosexuality, and, according to some Bible scholars, healed the lover of a gay Roman officer and commended the officer's faith.

In modern times, the followers of this more liberal "God" stand up for the rights of children, women, victims of discrimination, LGBT individuals, immigrants, the poor and the oppressed. They stand against private prisons, torture, the militarization of local police, and aggressive foreign policies that prefer war over diplomacy. They challenge the prison/military/industrial complex. They prefer criminal justice reform that emphasizes restitution, rehabilitation and restoration - rather than punishment.

In their minds, no man is an island. Any man's death diminishes the rest of us. Their motto is, "Leave no one behind." They question the concept of hell and believe in universal salvation.

Since politics is ultimately about economics, consider specifically what the liberal God of the Old Testament said about money and possessions. In the book of Ezekial, the prophet writes, "Behold, this was the guilt of your sister Sodom: she and her daughters had arrogance, abundant food, and careless ease, but she did not help the poor and needy. Woe to those who enact evil statutes, and to those who continually record unjust decisions, so as to deprive the needy of justice, and rob the poor of their rights."

In Deuteronomy, God instructed, "If there is a poor man among you in any of the towns of the land which the Lord your God is giving you, you shall not harden your heart, nor close your hand to your poor brother; but you shall freely open your hand to him, and generously lend him sufficient for his need in whatever he lacks. When you reap the harvest of your land, you shall not reap to the very corners of your field; you shall leave them for the needy and for the stranger. I am the LORD your God."

In another place, God said, "Open your mouth for the dumb, for the rights of all the unfortunate. Open your mouth, judge righteously, and defend the rights of the afflicted and needy. Is this not the fast which I choose, to let the oppressed go free, and break every yoke? Is it not to divide your bread with the hungry, and bring the homeless poor into the house; when you see the naked, to cover him, and not to hide yourself from your own flesh? Do justice and righteousness, and deliver the one who has been robbed from the power of his oppressor. Also, do not mistreat or do violence to the stranger, the orphan, or the widow."

It was this liberal version of God that inspired Jesus to say, "Sell your possessions and give to charity. Let the man with two tunics share with him who has none, and let him who has food do likewise. Give to him who asks of you, and do not turn away from him who wants to borrow from you. You cannot serve God and money."

In modern times, it's the followers of this liberal "God" that support Social Security, Medicare, Medicaid and other social safety nets for the poor and aged. They support universal healthcare, and they oppose tax cuts that primarily benefit the wealthy. They identify as "liberals", even though it leads to ridicule, persecution and sometimes even death. They speak truth to power and stand against all forms of political and economic exploitation.

They, too, become like their "God".

We humans easily fall into slavery and exploitation. Historically, it usually involves religion and economics. I trust you will ponder all I've shared in the first two sections of this book, and commit yourself to freedom.

I'm reminded of John Lennon's song, *Imagine*.

Imagine there's no countries.
It isn't hard to do.
Nothing to kill or die for,
And no religion, too.
Imagine all the people
Living life in peace...

Imagine no possessions.
I wonder if you can.
No need for greed or hunger,
A brotherhood of man.
Imagine all the people
Sharing all the world...

John Alan Shope

Freedom from Addiction

*"Imagine trying to live without air.
Now imagine something worse,"* Amy Reed

"An over-indulgence of anything, even something as pure as water, can intoxicate," Criss Jami

Regardless of how smart we are, how well educated we are or what we've experienced in life; we really only know one thing for sure. We can believe, speculate, meditate or pontificate all we want, but there's only one thing we really know beyond any doubt. It holds true for every one of us all the time. It is this.

Every day, you and I will pursue pleasure and try to avoid pain. We can make numerous predictions regarding what people will or will not think or do; but the only thing we know for sure is this: **every man, woman and child will pursue pleasure and resist pain, every moment of every day.**

We may define pleasure and pain differently, but pleasure and pain will drive everything we do. Even if you were to sacrifice your life for another person, it is because the sacrifice gave you some level of pleasure that outweighed the pain involved. You may try to resist this basic drive, but even that resistance is driven by the pleasure you experience from resisting.

A growing number of neurobiologists and anthropologists are suggesting that a desire for pleasure, rather than survival, drives evolution. As scientists delve deeper into the chemistry of life itself, pleasure producing molecules similar to dopamine appear to pre-date replicating molecules like RNA and DNA.

The Nature of Addiction

It is this inevitable pursuit of pleasure and the avoidance of pain that causes addiction. Here's what happens. Just like our planet, our body is a delicate ecosystem that requires a particular state of chemical balance to remain healthy. When our bodies are chemically imbalanced, we may feel pain or pleasure, depending on the particular chemicals involved. Long term stress, for example, causes high levels of cortisol, which can feel bad.

On the other hand, certain stimulates, physical and mental, cause high levels of chemicals called endorphins, which feel good. Endorphins include chemical neurotransmitters such as serotonin, dopamine and oxytocin. Low levels of these chemicals almost always feel bad, but high levels can feel very, very good. Obviously, humans devote a lot of time and energy, consciously and unconsciously, to physical and mental stimulates that cause high levels of endorphins.

But here's the catch. You build up tolerance. When confronted with excessive or long term chemical imbalance, your body adapts by releasing less of the particular chemicals causing the imbalance. This means that as you continue to stimulate your body to produce high levels of endorphins, your body gradually becomes less and less responsive in an attempt to maintain balance.

To keep experiencing the same pleasurable imbalance you experienced the first time you encountered a particular stimulate, you will have to keep increasing the stimulate. At this point, you're not addicted but you are building up tolerance.

When does tolerance become addiction? As you keep increasing the stimulate, your body will keep adapting by releasing less and less endorphins. Finally, even with the stimulate, your body will only be releasing the amount of endorphins it once released without the stimulate.

If you stop the stimulate at this point, your body now won't release enough endorphins for you to feel normal. Now you are experiencing addiction. **The stimulate no longer brings you pleasure; you need it just to feel normal.**

Now, you're in a very risky place. What if the stimulate starts causing problems in other parts of your body, or other areas of your life? If you stop the stimulate, you create a chemical imbalance that can feel extremely painful. If you don't stop, the other problem remains and may get worse. You are addicted to a stimulate that is causing pain when present, and is also causing pain when not present.

Food, alcohol, opiates, nicotine, sex, and money are among the most common stimulates that work in the manner described above. They initially create chemical imbalances that make us feel good. But if used excessively over time, our body becomes dependent on them, and we need them just to feel normal. Unfortunately, that dependency can cause other problems related to health, employment, family, etc.

The good news is that in most cases, your body can gradually re-adapt, so that you feel normal again without the stimulate. If you stop the stimulate, your body will gradually begin to release more endorphins on its own; but it may take awhile. Alcohol and drug counselors call this "recovery".

Most people can recover from most addictions, but it can be an extremely long and painful process, depending on the nature of the stimulate, the physical and mental makeup of the person, and the person's environment.

It's rare, but there are individuals for whom violence against other people triggers the release of endorphins. These broken and sick people seem to have problems that go beyond addiction. They clearly need to be in recovery; but sometimes full recovery is not possible. In those situations, some type of quarantine or confinement may be the only option. While the confinement is about public safety rather than punishment; it's still necessary. Fortunately, most addictions do not fall into that category.

We're all addicted to a variety of physical and mental stimulates. Many addictions are positive and sustainable, especially those that result in less sensitivity to pain, stronger muscles, less anxiety, marketable skills or healthy relationships. Healthy food, for example, could be viewed as an "addiction" that is both positive and sustainable.

But others are obviously negative and unsustainable. These addictions can oppress us and even possess us like mythical demons. They can destroy our lives, and the lives of those we care about.

While many struggle with destructive types of addiction, most of us are "functional addicts". In other words, our addictions aren't destroying our lives, but they are certainly making life far less enjoyable than it could be.

When religion talks about sin, it's talking about something very similar to addiction. But instead of being punished, as religion often suggests; what we need is healing and freedom.

Breaking Free

The only solution to a harmful addiction is to stop engaging in the addictive behavior. In most cases, the mind and body will slowly re-adapt and return to an earlier state of balance and freedom. But stopping can be difficult and complicated.

Some people, through no fault of their own, seem to be more susceptible to addiction than others. Genes, environment and various random events all play a role. It's easy to blame it all on bad choices, but it's far more complicated than that. Making good choices is harder for some than others, especially children and teenagers.

Wise teachers like Buddha and Jesus understood this. This is why their focus was on compassion and healing, rather than punishment. Unfortunately, we tend to approach addiction as a crime rather than a sickness. We need to see a bigger picture, re-think our approach and help people do the following.

Replacement

For most, the first step to freedom will be to replace the harmful addiction with a less harmful one. Alcohol and drugs, for example, can be replaced with less harmful substances. Unhealthy activities can be replaced with healthier activities.

Nature abhors a vacuum. When you take away something significant, you almost always need to replace it with something else. Otherwise, long term freedom is unlikely.

Most addictions involve more than just a single stimulate. One's entire environment can be part of the addictive process. To be free, one may have to change one's entire environment of people, places and things.

Identifying and removing the various entities that trigger a desire for addictive behavior is a crucial step. It will usually require radical changes in friends, routines, schedules and perhaps even employment. Some people find freedom through religion. The main reason this works is because it usually involves a major change in lifestyle and environment.

Moderation

The second step in freedom from addiction is to adopt a lifestyle based on moderation. Aristotle's famous "golden mean" reflects this emphasis in ancient Greek philosophy. Buddha encouraged a middle way between religious extremism and worldly indulgence. Similar teachings can be found in every culture. Our natural and often insatiable desire for pleasure must be tamed.

Unfortunately, humans tend to go from one extreme to the other. We learn the hard way. We see this in our politics as well as in our personal lives. The pendulum swings back and forth. This is true for all of us, but especially those of us with addictive personalities. We don't know when or where to stop.

Those of us with a degree of OCD also find it difficult to do things in moderation. Perfectionist tendencies encourage extremes. Many of us also go to unhealthy extremes because of stress and anxiety.

Our inability to fulfill our desires in moderation makes it difficult to avoid addictive behaviors. Freedom requires that we learn to wait, slow down, delay gratification, take breaks, and know when to say "that's enough". Crash diets and other extreme responses to over indulgence never work, because they are not based on a lifestyle of moderation.

Learning the value of moderation starts in childhood, but must be maintained throughout life. As adults, we are constantly bombarded with ads telling us to eat more, go more, buy more and indulge more. To not break away from the herd and adopt a simpler lifestyle will only lead to stress, fatigue and addiction.

There's an old saying, "Live simply so others can simply live". Adopting a simpler lifestyle will obviously benefit others; but it will also help you avoid addiction.

Nature teaches us to live moderately, if we listen. She never takes more than she needs. A tree only takes from the ground under its limbs. A lion only takes one calf from the herd it attacks, and leaves the rest. A bee only takes the pollen it needs, without harming the rest of the flower.

Only humans leave such a wide path of destruction due to our greed and our inability to be content. When something does that within our own bodies, we call it cancer and try to remove it before it kills us. Moderation is the second key to finding and maintaining freedom.

Detachment or Letting Go

Replacing harmful addictions with healthier ones and learning to live more moderately are crucial to personal freedom and long term happiness. The ultimate cure for addiction, however, is detachment. In other words, the ultimate path to freedom requires knowing when and how let go.

Most of us depend on various physical or mental stimulates to trigger the release of pleasurable endorphins. As described above, alcohol, drugs, sex, money, food and other "pleasurable" behaviors are common triggers.

What most people are not aware of, however, is a deep feeling of pleasure that does not require physical or mental stimulation. Many discover this through meditation. People who meditate regularly often experience the release of numerous endorphins, without a triggering stimulate of any kind.

There are numerous ways to meditate. Walking or running can be done meditatively. During traditional meditation, one normally focuses on one's breathing, so as to not focus on anything else. Random thoughts and feelings still occur; but rather than resist or dwell on them, one simply notices them and lets them fade away. Surprisingly, during this state of mental emptiness - self induced sensory deprivation - your body releases numerous endorphins. You experience a deep state of natural pleasure, independent of any specific trigger. QiGong is another yoga type practice that integrates both mind and body to achieve a similar state of pleasurable relaxation.

With practice, this non-stimulated state of bliss can last beyond your meditation session and make every moment of life more pleasurable. Meditation ultimately becomes an attitude. You begin to live a life characterized by detachment and a growing ability to let go when needed. Instead of acquiring and possessing, you begin downsize and let go. Over time, this growing sense of natural contentment allows you to live more simply and be free from addictive substances, possessions and behaviors.

Spontaneous Healing

I would be remiss if I did not mention those who seem to have experienced instantaneous freedom from addiction through some type of "spiritual" experience. I have a good friend, Larry, who found immediate and permanent (at least after several years and still counting) freedom from alcohol during a simple prayer. Several others have made similar claims to me regarding their addiction to other drugs.

The fact that one "spiritual" experience could accomplish what usually occurs after years of therapy and continued group support raises the possibility that there is more to human existence than the physical world we experience day to day. I will discuss this more fully later in the book.

Top 5 Addictions

Humans, more than most animals, tend to do things in excess. Humans, more than most animals, tend to experience addiction. Humans, more than most animals, must learn to enjoy life responsibly, and know how and when to let go. Some behaviors are far more addictive than others. Here are some of those wonderful, yet dangerous, behaviors that need to be approached carefully and moderately in order to achieve and maintain freedom.

Money & Stuff

My dad never made a lot of money. He never owned a home or a new car. He worked hard, but always lived paycheck to paycheck. He never got ahead financially, and I remember many times when he was completely broke. But I never met anyone that was happier or freer than my dad. Among the many things he taught me, one was that "stuff" doesn't make you happy.

According to the Bible, Jesus said, "Happy are you poor!" Happy are those who have learned to resist greed and the false promises of material wealth - the false idea that more "stuff" means more happiness. Jesus talked about giving away possessions and not worrying about what to wear or what to eat. While modern Christianity rarely emphasizes it, it was at the heart of Jesus' message.

St. Francis of Assisi followed the teachings of Jesus more fully than most. He gave up his inheritance and fell in love with who he called, "Lady Poverty". He gave away all his wealth and possessions. The peace and happiness he subsequently found has been the subject of countless books, poems and movements.

I'm not suggesting that everyone fall in love with
"Lady Poverty" or join a commune; although thousands have found it deeply satisfying. I am suggesting that we all recognize the dangers and the deceitfulness of wealth. As so many enlightened teachers have taught over the centuries, "a man's life does not consist of his possessions".

We all know people who slaved all their life to acquire wealth. Then, when they finally decided to retire and start enjoying their wealth, they experienced health issues that prevented them from doing so. I know many, myself included, who down-sized and decided to live with less so they could enjoy life more. I highly recommend it.

Again, everyone's situation is different, and many have no choice but to keep working well into old age, but far too many sell their soul to the almighty dollar and later regret it. Most Americans would do well to live more simply, avoid debt when possible and not let money become their master.

We all need a minimum amount of financial security to be happy. But beyond that, we quickly discover the law of diminishing returns. Happiness does not increase relative to the amount of money and stuff we have. Often, there's even an inverse relationship. Over the years, I've known many who had far less wealth than me, but were enjoying life far more.

I personally know two families from France who quit their jobs, moved with their young children to the US and lived among the poor for 2 years. They did it under the supervision of an organization that helped them work out the details, but once they were here, they lived in complete solidarity with and experienced the same poverty as those around them. They lived in similar houses, ate similar food and had little money. Although they were able to help their neighbors in some ways, they would be the first to say they received far more than they gave. They discovered a level of freedom they had not known before.

How many young people choose careers based on money rather than happiness? How many young people lock themselves into a life time of debt and a job they hate, just to have a bigger house or a newer car? How foolish is our society for saddling our young people with overwhelming student debt? How foolish are all of us for allowing politicians to weaken safety nets and retirement options that most of us will depend on, whether we think we will or not?

The next time you receive a pay raise you could live without, would you consider giving it to someone who needs it much more? My point is simply that you may find there really is more joy and freedom in giving than receiving. You may discover that when it comes to money and "stuff", less really is more.

I talked earlier of economic exploitation and how we should all work for economic justice and equality by supporting more liberal economic policies. The ultimate way to avoid economic exploitation is to not follow the herd and learn to be content with less. Money is addictive. It starts out making you happy but then enslaves you. Learn to let go early and often.

Greed may very well destroy our species. As someone wisely stated regarding the Earth's resources, there is more than enough for all our need, but not nearly enough for all our greed.

Sex

Like money, sex is both wonderful and dangerous. Unfortunately, our culture, influenced by religion, often forces us to extremes of either repression or indulgence. Young people are going to explore their sexuality with or without permission or education. As young adults continue to postpone getting married, or even abandon the idea completely, traditional approaches to sex no longer make sense.

No one ever made a worse decision because they had too much information. That's especially true with sex. Forcing people to repress normal and healthy sexual desires always backfires.

Morality cannot be legislated. What consenting adults do behind closed doors is none of our business, as long as no one is being hurt, harassed or exploited. Our society needs to have honest and practical conversation regarding sex. And it needs to be science based rather than religion based.

I'm not suggesting we have no rules or laws to protect each other, especially women and children. We need to confront all the subtle ways in which our society harasses and exploits women. And women need to be part of the process; not just a bunch of old white men, which is too often the case. Thankfully, those who harass and exploit in our society, especially men in power, are being called out and held responsible more and more often. I hope this trend continues.

Children, by definition, cannot consent; therefore they must be protected everywhere and always. Those who sexually exploit or molest children must be stopped. Are there gray areas? Sure. A 17 year old having sex with a 15 year old is obviously different than a 30 year old having sex with a 15 year old.

Most child molesters were molested themselves as children. They, too, are sick and broken people who need healing. Unfortunately, research suggests that many cannot be healed and must be quarantined in some way. We need wise judges who can take all this into consideration. Still, children must be protected, and it's always better to err on the side of protection.

Should prostitution be legalized? It's a valid question. Forcing activities underground and creating a black market seldom works. Just like with drugs, criminals are usually the only ones who benefit. On the other hand, young people are vulnerable to exploitation, especially if they are uneducated and poor. Again, we need to have an honest and open conversation, based on scientific data rather than religion.

Like money, sex is a wonderful servant but a horrible master. Like volatile explosives, it must be handled with care. Understanding the principle of "delayed gratification", having the ability to say "no", having the knowledge to make responsible decisions, recognizing addictive patterns and knowing when and how to "let go" are all things that will preserve our sexual freedom and well being.

Alcohol & Drugs

We've talked about alcohol already. Like sex, it's been both a blessing and a curse from the beginning. Like sex, we need to avoid the extremes of repression and over indulgence. Education is the key. My experience is that young adults should learn to drink responsibly from their parents, rather than their buddies at school. Again, scientific data is a better teacher than religion.

My years in criminal justice clearly taught me that alcohol and drug addiction should be treated as diseases not crimes. Private prisons and others who exploit the problem for money or political gain will obviously disagree, but the research is clear.

In my humble opinion, drug possession should be decriminalized. The war on drugs has failed, and that money will be much better spent on rehabilitation. DUIs and DWIs should be heavily fined, but they should not result in criminal charges, time in jail or loss of employment. Many European nations take this approach and it seems to work.

As mentioned earlier, religion has helped many alcoholics and drug addicts find freedom. AA and inpatient recovery programs have helped far more. Prison and the resulting loss of employment opportunities only make matters worse.

Once again, education and radical changes in environment and lifestyle are keys to successful recovery. Teaching our children to enjoy things in moderation and making sure they understand the dynamics of addiction are keys to preserving freedom.

Food

As in the case of money, sex and alcohol; books have been written teaching us how to eat healthy. My goal here is simply to share a few basic principles in the context of finding and maintaining freedom.

At dinner one evening, I asked my friends from France how most Europeans saw Americans. After listing several things they admired about America, they finally gave me this short but revealing answer to my original question: "soldiers and fat".

After leaving the field of criminal justice, I spent several years ghost writing for several medical doctors. I enjoyed the research it forced me to do. I found the medical research associating diet with disease overwhelming. More and more doctors are discovering the role of food in causing and curing disease. We are what we eat.

The principles are actually very simple.

Don't over eat. In other words don't feel you have to eat everything on your plate. American restaurants serve far bigger portions than most other countries. It may not help the economy, but you will live longer (and save money) if you share meals at restaurants when possible. Leave the same tip you would leave if you ordered 2 meals, however. Your waiter or waitress is working just as hard.

Eat far more vegetables and fruits than meats. Know that organic and grass fed meats are healthier than regular meats. It's worth the extra money, and if more people will make that choice, prices should come down.

The more colorful your food; the more nutritious it is. Again organic is best, especially regarding the well known "dirty dozen" foods that absorb far more pesticides than other vegetables and fruits. Choose NON-GMO vegetables when possible. The main concern with GMOs is the possibility they contain too much pesticide and other chemicals which threaten human hormonal function. As always, do the research and make sure your sources are non-biased.

Minimize sugar. Most don't realize how much sugar they consume in beverages. I live in the south where sweet tea is rampant. If your addicted to sweet tea, you will be surprised how quickly you can adjust to half and half, and then ultimately to unsweet, with just a shot of sweet on top.

According to the CDC, almost one third of the US population will be diabetic by the year 2050 if we don't change our relationship with sugar. Read labels and track your sugar intake.

Choose healthy fats. A recent study involving olive oil found that one group replacing all their fat with extra virgin olive reduced their risk of heart attack by 40%. The well known Mediterranean diet draws much of its benefit from its focus on vegetables and high quality extra virgin olive oil.

Avocado is another good fat. Low mercury fish such as salmon and sardines are important sources of heart healthy fat. Again, pay attention to quality and prefer wild caught sources.

More and more Americans are developing sensitivity to dairy and wheat. Many find their health greatly improves after they become gluten free or dairy free. Again, do the research and be smart.

What about supplements? Quality matters and varies greatly, even within the same brand. Over supplementing can be as problematic as the deficiency you are trying to resolve. It's always better to get your nutrition from food rather than a supplement, unless a deficiency is clearly diagnosed and food is not enough. When possible, base your use of supplements on blood tests.

Having said that, let me suggest that a quality supplement may sometimes be a better option than a prescription drug; but please talk with your doctor before making any change. America is one of only two developed countries allowing pharmaceuticals to advertise. Too much of our healthcare system is driven by money. Keep that in mind.

As mentioned earlier, food is very addictive, especially sugar and unhealthy fat. Recognize addictive patterns and practice letting go of unhealthy foods and habits. A brief period of meditation will often take away the desire for a late night snack, or at least allow you to choose a healthier option.

Eat slowly. You may be surprised how many digestive problems can be healed by eating less and eating slowly.

Finally, consider occasional and moderate fasting. I'm not suggesting that you fast for days. That can be dangerous and needs to be done under medical supervision. But numerous studies related to less intense fasting show significant promise. Cutting back to 500 calories one or two days per week may provide several medical benefits for many people. Calorie restricted diets seem to increase longevity. Again, do some research and talk with your health care provider.

Anger

Anger is not an addiction, but like an addiction, destructive anger can be managed by learning to let go. Anger is normal and healthy when expressed in a healthy non-violent manner. But some people have anger issues, perhaps stemming from childhood or other chemical imbalances. Losing control of one's temper is always problematic, whether it results in physical or emotional violence.

Parents especially should control their anger in front of their kids. Remember that everything is magnified in the ears and mind of a child. Yelling can be just as harmful as a violent strike in the face. For some, anger management courses can be extremely valuable and life changing. If you were yelled at or abused by a parent, please get help and break the cycle.

Often, the cure for anger is forgiveness. Forgiveness is simply another form of letting go. Forgiveness is not for the benefit of the person being forgiven. Forgiveness is for the benefit of the forgiver. Buddha said, "Holding on to anger is like drinking poison and expecting the other person to die."

People hurt people. Usually, it's due to blindness or some other brokenness in the person doing the harm. Understanding that can make it easier to forgive. I'm reminded of what Jesus said while dying on the cross, "Father, forgive them, they do not know what they are doing." Even at death, Jesus benefitted from the forgiveness far more than his assailants.

Remember, you never forgive because the person said they were sorry or changed in some way. Ultimately, it's not about them. You forgive because you need to let go of the hurt. You forgive because you - not them - need to be free.

Again, express your anger non-violently, and, when appropriate, let the person who hurt you know how you feel. Talk about your anger with a trusted friend or counselor. But then let it go. Forgiveness is a process, and it may take awhile. Nevertheless, let it go, let it go, let it go.

Conclusion

You never know when a desire will lead to an addiction. To maintain freedom, practice detachment. Detachment was at the heart of Buddha's and Jesus' message. Buddha taught that all suffering is the result of desire. He concluded that detachment from desire is the ultimate solution to suffering. He taught his followers to "let go", not just during meditation, but everywhere and always.

"Be here now" is a common saying among Buddhists. It means to let go of somewhere else, yesterday and tomorrow. The present space and present moment are all you really have. Be still, be free and just be, right here, right now.

Everything is temporary. This is a good thing, because everything bad that could happen might, but it won't last forever. Impermanence is a built in safety net.

On the flip side, good things won't last forever either. All the various things we get addicted too will someday be taken away from us. Learning to let go today will make that future day less painful.

The moon waxes…
The moon wanes…
The moon waxes…
The moon wanes…
I am the moon.

Freedom from Fear

Most of this section focuses on the fear associated with death. But I want to begin by saying a few words about fears associated with childhood events.

Painful Childhood Events

"I have accepted fear as part of life – specifically the fear of change... I have gone ahead despite the pounding in the heart that says: turn back," Erica Jong

We all fear many things. Most of our fears come from deep within our subconscious. They are often rooted in painful childhood events that our mind may have forgotten, but our body never did. Science continues to discover strong links between disease and painful memories deep below our conscious awareness.

Painful events in our past drive most of our insecurities, our anger, our need to control and our feeling of not being loved. It doesn't matter how real the events were. Perception is reality, and what we believed and felt at the time will continue to haunt us until we become free from it.

I've had the good fortune to know many gifted people who taught me far more than I could ever learn in books. Don't get me wrong. I've read more books than I can begin to remember, and I highly recommend you devote at least as much time to reading good books as you do to watching the TV monitor or interacting with Facebook. But, also, have as many conversations as you can with smart and gifted people.

One such person is a physical therapist I know near Orlando, Florida. Kevin and Robyn Rose help people recover from painful events buried deep within their sub-conscious. Kevin uses wild animals to help returning vets recover from PTSD. Robin uses Cranial Sacral Therapy and other techniques to identify and release painful childhood memories that cause physical and emotional distress in adulthood.

I first visited Robyn at the insistence of my daughter. At the time, I was experiencing occasional depression and anxiety following a major career change. Stomach issues that I had struggled with since childhood also seemed to be getting worse. My wife and I had recently moved to Florida. This obviously added to the stress, but there was more beneath the surface.

To make a long story short, over several therapy sessions, Robyn took me back to various times in my childhood when I had been hurt or scared. Each time, she would ask me, "What would you say to your younger self right now?" As I began to speak to my younger self, a flood of emotion and tears burst forth and I felt a deep calmness and peace I had not felt in many years.

I, along with many others, experienced significant emotional healing as Robyn helped us revisit and resolve painful childhood events. Some of the events seem silly as I think about them now, but to a young child they were very painful and enduring.

Not everyone has access to someone like Robyn, but simply realizing that much of our fear stems from forgotten or repressed childhood events can be a first step toward healing and freedom for many. Explore self-help books. Take advantage of counseling. Seek out community support groups. Sometimes, just talking about specific childhood events with family members or a friend can do wonders.

There is a vast array of self-hypnosis resources on the internet that can also help. Try several until you find one that feels safe and promising. As always, if you are being treated for depression, anxiety or other mental discomfort, talk with your healthcare provider before engaging in any type of self treatment. Any activity that makes you feel worse should be stopped immediately and only continued under professional supervision.

Finally, during periods of meditation, listen to the child that still lives within you. Great wisdom teachers often talk about the child within. Much of our fear stems from childhood. For many, that's the first place to go on a journey toward freedom from fear.

John Alan Shope

Fear of Death

One of the fathers of modern psychology, Sigmund Freud, believed that a desire for sex and a fear of death drive almost everything we do. We all fear death. Death is the ultimate "letting go". Most religiosity stems from a fear of death. A near death experience can be life changing.

My life was heavily influenced by early encounters with death. They included the death of my dad's uncle Bob, the violent death of a dog, a teenage neighbor who died in a car wreck, a friend shot to death simply for being at the wrong place at the wrong time, the death of my first girl friend, Sharon, in a car wreck, and the death of my sister, Pam, in a car wreck shortly thereafter. All these occurred before I turned 22.

These deaths were followed by the deaths of young people and old people in churches I served during my early adulthood. My wife's breast cancer when she was 35 was another powerful reminder that death is always nearby. Then later, I lost my brother, Phil. Most recently, I lost my mom and dad.

Death is part of life. The older you get, the more reminders there are. Your own body begins to wear out as more and more friends and relatives are diagnosed with cancer and heart disease.

It was early encounters with death and suffering that started Buddha on his search for "enlightenment". His parents tried to hide the realities of disease and death from him, but to no avail. How does one come to terms with death and find freedom from the fear it creates?

Coming to Terms with Death

When I first heard John Lennon's song, *Imagine*, I was both inspired and bothered.

"Imagine there's no heaven,
It's easy if you try.
No hell below us;
Above us only sky."

No heaven? Religious notions of "heaven" give people hope in the face of death. For millions, taking away that hope and raising the possibility that this life is all there is, only adds to their fear. The church seduces you by promising that heaven is real and you can go there when you die, along with your loved ones, as long as you meet certain conditions.

Unfortunately, truth and freedom require that you reject such religious dishonesty and acknowledge that no one really knows for sure what may or may not happen after we die.

In the pages that follow, I will suggest three healthier ways to approach death: 1) focus more on life, 2) broaden your sense of "self", 3) explore the mystery of human consciousness.

The Gift of Life

"It is not death that a man should fear, but he should fear never beginning to live," Marcus Aurelius

Many claim they do not fear death itself. Rather, they fear the process of dying, which is often painful. I'm sure there's a lot of truth in that, but I think our fear of death involves more than just the process of dying.

To various degrees, we are all addicted to life. Life is a wonderful party full of activities we enjoy and people we love. Death is being asked to leave the party and the people, and let it continue without you. That's a tough thing to do. Surprisingly, many people seem to have made peace with it.

My good friend, Danny, is one of those who seems to have come to terms with death regardless of what it entails. Many years ago, during my Baptist preacher years, I said to him, "If this life is all there is, I would rather not have been born. God can have it back."

In hindsight, I realize I sounded like a spoiled child. Even the Bible asks, "Shall what is formed say to the one who formed it, 'Why did you make me like this?'" As years went by, I gradually accepted the possibility that this life may be all there is – we just don't know.

While accepting that reality, however, I also became grateful for what we do know – we are alive right now. That there is something rather than nothing may be the greatest miracle of all. To get to experience it, even if just for a little while, is, in some ways, like winning the lottery.

Some say there is no free lunch. Our life on Earth is a free lunch and we should be grateful for the meal. I regularly remind myself how wonderful it is to be alive today and to be part of something so beautiful and amazing, regardless of what the future brings.

My brother, Phil, went through some rough times toward the end of his life. He felt a lot of emotional pain, especially with regard to his family.

But shortly before he died, he found the strength and clarity to say, "It didn't turn out like I planned, but overall it was a good ride."

My dad had a similar attitude throughout his life. One of his favorite responses to a problem was, "No big deal." It used to irritate me, but as I got older, I understood where he was coming from. His problems seemed to always pale in comparison to just being alive.

Far too many view life as a problem to be solved, a curse to be broken, a fallen world to be saved from. Life is a gift, a playground, an adventure and a party. Life is not a problem to be solved. It's is a gift to be enjoyed. Life is a game, but it's not about winning or losing; it's simply about getting to play. There is no original sin crying out for redemption. You don't have to fix anything or pass a test or figure anything out.

Life is a roller coaster. You face a challenge, and then you experience peace. Then, you face another challenge, followed by another season of peace. The rhythm continues like the seasons, as you learn to engage and then let go, engage and then let go, over and over again. You can learn to manage and even enjoy this natural cycle of pleasure and pain. You can finally be grateful that you got to take the ride.

The fear of death causes millions of people to see the universe as unfriendly, judgmental, cruel and threatening. Religion exploits that fear. But a growing number of people see the universe as friendly, safe, inviting and exciting. Having broken free from religion, they have accepted their mortality and allowed their obsession with life to overcome their fear of death.

Trust the mystery. Let go and release yourself, fully and unconditionally, to what is. Enjoy right here, right now.

Why is there something rather than nothing? It just is. Why is there suffering? It just is. Why are you here? You just are. Embrace the mystery of life. Stop trying to control everything. Learn from the past, plan for future, but don't stress over any of it. Learn to go with the flow. Accept your destiny. Learn to say with a smile, "Maybe, maybe not, I wonder."

A good friend of mine, Woody Burt, who started out as a Baptist preacher and ended up being president of a college, used to tell the story of 2 knights sent out by a king to explore the kingdom. One was commanded to report back on all the good things he saw. The other was commanded to report back on all the bad things he saw.

When they returned, the king commanded the one sent to look for the bad, "Tell me all the good you saw." He replied, "I saw no good; I was looking for the bad." Then the king commanded the knight sent to look for the good "Tell me all the bad you saw." He replied, "I saw no bad; I was looking for the good."

The lesson is simple. We find what we look for. If we focus on death, we won't enjoy life. If we focus on life and all the good things in life, we can accept whatever death entails.

The Bible contains a good piece of advice in the last part of Paul's letter to the church at Philippi. "Finally, brethren, whatever is true, whatever is honorable, whatever is right, whatever is pure, whatever is lovely, whatever is of good repute, if there is any excellence and if anything worthy of praise, dwell on these things."

I think we can all accept the possibility of no afterlife, if we have to. Most of us will go through a grieving process - denial, bargaining, anger and depression - before we finally reach acceptance. Ultimately, however, we can accept what is and even become grateful for what is. We can make peace with death and begin to focus on life - perhaps more so than ever before.

Moments of Exceptional Bliss

In the movie, *Midnight in Paris*, there is a scene in which Ernest Hemingway speaks of death. While they capture some of his style, Hemingway never actually wrote the words. Nevertheless, the words reveal a truth that speaks to many. Here's the full quote.

"All men fear death. It's a natural fear that consumes us all. We fear death because we feel that we haven't loved well enough or loved at all, which ultimately are one and the same. However, when you make love with a truly great woman, one that deserves the utmost respect in this

world and one that makes you feel truly powerful, that fear of death completely disappears. Because when you are sharing your body and heart with a great woman the world fades away. You two are the only ones in the entire universe. You conquer what most lesser men have never conquered before, you have conquered a great woman's heart, the most vulnerable thing she can offer to another.

Death no longer lingers in the mind. Fear no longer clouds your heart. Only passion for living, and for loving, become your sole reality. This is no easy task for it takes insurmountable courage. But remember this, for that moment when you are making love with a woman of true greatness you will feel immortal. I believe that love that is true and real creates a respite from death.

All cowardice comes from not loving or not loving well, which is the same thing. And when the man who is brave and true looks death squarely in the face like some rhino hunters I know or Belmonte, who is truly brave, it is because they love with sufficient passion to push death out of their minds. Until it returns, as it does to all men. And then you must make really good love again. Think about it."

Occasionally, we have an experience that is so wonderful and perfect, that it would be ok if our whole life was simply about having that one experience - and nothing else. It may or may not involve making love. Regardless of the context, if you were to die right then, it would be OK.

I've had a few such experiences. I had one several years ago with my wife. Afterwards, nothing else mattered. Life was complete. Death was irrelevant. Obviously, those experiences are rare and the feelings fade; but there are times when life overwhelms death and removes the fear. Rather than run from death, seek those moments in life.

Ethics without Religion

Some may wonder: if this life is all there is, does it matter how we live? Of course it does! Some have the silly idea that without a God in heaven to judge, or a religion to guide, we will all become worthless and horrible people.

To the contrary, some of the kindest and most moral people I know do not believe in God and have no use for religion. They simply know that we're all connected and we all do better when we all do better. You don't have to live in poverty to be affected by other people's poverty. It doesn't take a lot of intelligence to finally figure out that seeking pleasure at other people's expense hurts us all in the long run. What goes around come around. We naturally reap what we sow.

History teaches us the value of fairness and the dangers of selfishness and greed. Plato's four cardinal virtues of wisdom, courage, moderation and justice were rooted in philosophy, not religion. The Code of Hammurabi, an ancient Babylonian code of law, covered far more ground than the Bible's 10 Commandments and pre-dated them. The ethical writings of Confucius were based on reason and logic.

Values such as truth, equality, justice, kindness and mercy are the product of evolution, not divine revelation. From a historical perspective, religion has stood in the way of justice and goodness far more often than it has promoted them.

Beyond common sense and practicality, most human beings possess empathy. We feel the pain of those around us - our spouses, our children, siblings, extended family, friends and hopefully many others. Who among us isn't touched by the suffering of children and adults in other parts of the world?

When we are made aware of their plight, we feel their pain. Hopefully, most of us feel the pain of animals. We possess traits such as empathy and love because such traits were necessary for our survival as a species. Today, modern psychology considers lack of empathy a mental illness.

Ethics and morality are based on giving value to certain ideas. Science values truth, evidence, logic, dialogue, self-criticism and open mindedness. These values have done far more good in the world than religious values. In fact, religion only makes progress when it allows these values to supersede faith and dogma.

My love for my wife and children does not depend on faith in God or belief in a soul. If science proves someday that my children are just a collection of chemicals interacting with their environment in a way that creates a temporary sense of self, that proof will not diminish my love for them or make them any less amazing.

Love and empathy will continue regardless of whether various religious claims are true or not. We will all grieve over and deeply miss our loved ones who die regardless of whether we are religious or not. But most of us will gradually make peace with the loss, regardless of whether we are religious or not.

The bottom line is this. As we learn to accept the reality of death and focus on life, we will become better at living. Free from concerns about heaven, we will focus on making earth a better place. We won't wait for a messiah from heaven to fix things – we'll work together to fix what we can right now.

Our fear of death will gradually give way to a grateful appreciation for life, even a mortal one. We will enjoy it as fully and responsibly as we can. But then we will let go – and be thankful for the ride.

The Wave

I watch the waves slowly rise, then peak, crash and fade.
Where do they come from? Where do they go?
Why do they appear at all?
They arise out of the great sea that is always and everywhere.
They return to that same great sea,
Only to rise again, in another place and another time.
They arise to play...with the surfers, the gulls, the wind
And me, as I lose myself in their beauty, their ever changing form
and their mystery.
They humbly and gratefully fill the space
Between the eternal depths and the ever changing world above.
As I wade further and further from the shore to catch my ride,
I lose myself in the moment,
And realize that I am that wave.

A Larger Sense of Self

Lennon's *Imagine* continues,

"You may say I'm a dreamer,
But I'm not the only one.
I hope someday you'll join us,
And the world will live as one."

What does it mean to "live as one"? Basically, it suggests that we broaden our sense of "self" to include all "selves". It goes beyond treating others as we want to be treated. It implies seeing our self in others and seeing others in our self – truly and continually feeling each other's joy and pain. To the degree that we can identify with other people, part of us continues to live through them after we die, and our fear of death decreases.

This is especially true regarding our children. The early parts of the Bible did not have much focus on an afterlife. Abraham, the spiritual father of Jews, Christians and Muslims, saw his immortality in his descendents. That's why it was such a wonderful miracle for his wife, Sarah, to give birth at an old age.

Think about your sense of "self". You start out in life connected to your mother. She and you share the same physical body for 9 months.

But at birth you begin to disconnect, physically and mentally. Your individuality begins to dominate and you develop a strong ego. You still care about family and friends, but you also enjoy the freedom of being a separate and independent self.

Then you fall in love and perhaps have children. Suddenly, you feel connected again. Your partner becomes part of you. Your children become an extension of you. Their futures become as important, if not more important, than yours. You may also develop special friendships along the way. All these relationships expand your sense of self.

Experiencing this larger sense of self is not limited to family and friends. A small group of soldiers can develop the same oneness. It then becomes easy for any one of them to sacrifice his or her own life for the rest of the group. Those who devote their lives to groups of people experiencing devastating poverty or disease develop the same deep solidarity.

As we journey through life, other people become part of who we are. When they die, a part of us dies with them. The more we can identify with other people, share our life with them, fall in love with them and join our destinies to theirs; the larger our sense of self becomes. Our small, individual "self" begins to die as a larger "self" emerges.

Psychologist, Carl Jung, gave us a valuable framework within which to better understand the **various levels of "self"**. The small "self", or ego, is your normal waking consciousness. This is the "self" you are normally aware of.

Below that, however, is your subconscious where a lifetime of memories are stored and processed, especially memories from childhood. This is a much larger "self" that you are, for the most part, unaware of. Even though you're not aware of it, this sub-conscious "self", drives most of how you feel and behave.

But "self" doesn't end there. Beyond your small conscious "self" and your larger subconscious "self", is a much, much larger "self" which Jung calls the collective unconscious. Jung was convinced that this part of you contained not just your memories, but the memories of your ancestors and, perhaps, the entire human race. This larger "self" transcends time and space and connects us all at a very deep level.

It's interesting that Buddha taught, 2500 years ago, that our small conscious "self" is somewhat of an illusion. Modern psychology agrees. It can't be physically located in the brain. You're not born with it, and it seems to be as much a product of cultural conditioning as anything else.

If you go, mentally, to that place beyond your small conscious "self" and beyond your sub-conscious "self", and begin to experience your larger "collective unconscious"; you will realize, first hand, that your small conscious "self" doesn't really define who you actually are. The apparent separation between you and everything else is somewhat of an illusion.

Everything is ultimately one thing, constantly changing and evolving; and you are simply part of that one bigger thing, which always was, always is and always will be. Experiencing this larger "self" allows you to move toward what many in the Eastern hemisphere refer to as enlightenment.

Many claim to transcend their small self and experience a much larger self during periods of deep meditation. As stated earlier, during meditation, the goal is to let go of all thoughts, feelings and sensations — all the things that constitute the ego or small self.

Again, many do this by focusing on their breath. As thoughts randomly arise, they are gently allowed to fade away, without resisting, judging or dwelling on them. Over time and with practice, one can experience an empty state of mind which allows one to transcend the small self and experience a larger self.

The poet, William Blake, must have had a similar experience when he wrote about "seeing the world in a grain of sand and heaven in a wild flower, holding infinity in the palm of your hand and eternity in an hour".

I've occasionally experienced bliss so full and complete I momentarily lost all desires and had no fear of death. Such moments transcend the smaller self. There are numerous books and websites that can teach you how to meditate and glimpse this bigger picture of who you are.

We have already discussed Jesus' teachings regarding dying to our small self and discovering a larger self. Here are a few more statements attributed to Jesus in the Bible, which seem to point in that direction.

"Do not fear him who can kill the body...Those who believe as me will live even if they die and whoever lives by believing as me will never die"

(John 11:25)[8]. Or the following, "Whoever hears my word...has eternal life... has crossed over from death to life" (John 5:23).

This idea of a larger self probably underlies Jesus' injunction to "not worry about your life, what you shall wear or what you shall eat." In other words, you are so much more than your physical body. You are part of everything around you.

When Jesus said, "The Kingdom of God is within you", he seems to be talking about this larger self waiting to be discovered. Rather than traditional ideas of salvation, discovering the larger self seems to be the "narrow road" and the "treasure hidden in a field" that Jesus encouraged people to follow and find.

From an ethical or moral perspective, our small self "misses the mark", which is the literal meaning of the word "sin". It keeps us selfish, blind, unhappy and very afraid of death. An expanded sense of self allows you to care more for others and wear life like a loose jacket. It encourages you to smile, laugh, let go, not worry, enjoy the moment and share.

Ernest Hemingway wrote, "Fear of death increases in exact proportion to increase in wealth". It seems that the more we have, the harder it is to let go at death. Wealth and possessions tend to strengthen our small self and feed our ego.

Sharing and having less tends to weaken our ego and reveal our larger self, connecting us more deeply with other people. Perhaps, that's why Buddha, Jesus and other wise teachers encouraged us to travel lightly and live simply.

Those who discover their larger self, by living more simply, meditating more regularly and connecting with others more deeply, seem to enjoy life more and fear death less. John Alan Shope will die, but my larger self will never die. A bigger "me" will continue living through my children and other living things.

Years ago, I began to realize this and I wrote these words:

---

[8] Most Bibles translate this verse, "believe **in** me", but the Greek phrase used here and in other places can just as easily be translated "believe **as** me".

"Someday, my green eyes will no longer see;
But my brown eyes will watch eternity."

I was thinking, not only of my children who all have their mother's brown eyes, but also of the one eternal essence we all share.

We are more than the physical bodies we inhabit. We are more than our small egos. Our egos make us feel separate from everything else, but much of that is an illusion. To experience the oneness of everything goes a long way toward freeing us from the fear of death.

The Tree of Life

The Tree of Life produces leaves
Of every shape and size.
They provide
Beauty,
Shade,
And food.

They are born in the spring,
Thrive in the summer,
Show off in the fall
And die in the winter.

The cycle continues
Year after year.
Challenged by disease
Drought
And natural events,
But never defeated.

You are a leaf.
Evolving and experiencing
The mystery and magic of life,
As a loved one, a stranger, an enemy.
Sometimes an animal or a plant.

You often think the leaf
Is all you are,
But you are every leaf.
A trillion leaves,
Spreading forth adventure
And love.

So sprout forth in the spring,
Share your beauty,
Provide shade,
Bear fruit.

But then
As winter approaches,
Let go
And fall to the ground

But remember:
The Tree never dies.
And if you reach high enough,
Beyond leaf and limb,
Beyond thoughts,
Feelings,
Sensations
And memories,

You will know:
You are just a leaf,
For a little while.
But you always were
And always will be
The Tree.

One Tree
With no beginning
And no end.
Incarnating a trillion times
In every leaf.

Consciousness – the Final Frontier

"Nothing in life is to be feared, it is only to be understood. Now is the time to understand more, so that we may fear less," Marie Curie

Over time, we can accept our mortality and begin to focus more fully on the life we have now. With practice we can expand our sense of self, experience the oneness we all share, and take comfort in a more communal (less personal) type of immortality. We will certainly benefit from such freedom.

But what if there's more to the story? What if a more personal aspect of who we are survives death in some yet-to-be-understood way? Our discussion of death would not be complete without an exploration of human consciousness.

There are two worlds in which humans live. One is a physical world of touching, seeing, tasting, smelling, hearing, feeling and processing chemical data – the various physical events facilitated by chemical reactions within our nervous systems.

The other world is a mental world of thinking, comprehending, imagining and just being aware. It seems to involve processes that go beyond chemicals and neurons.

The first world involves physical processes in the body that can be fairly well understood and tracked. The second world, while interacting with physical processes, seems to reach beyond the physical realm into areas of mental awareness and consciousness that remain somewhat of a mystery to modern science and medicine.

 Computers can recognize the color red, for example, when programmed with appropriate code, but only humans can actually comprehend the concept of color.

Science is still struggling to understand what it means to be conscious – to be aware and to comprehend. Pure awareness may be something like the following.

Take a moment to Imagine no physical sensations such as sight, sound, touch, smell or taste. Then, go further and imagine no emotions, no thoughts, no memories and no mental imagery of any kind. What's left?

Pure, empty awareness; pure, empty consciousness. This pure state of awareness, with no mental or emotional content whatsoever, is what I'm referring to in this section when I use the terms "consciousness", "field of conscious awareness" or "universal consciousness".

Traditionally, neurologists have believed that consciousness is a mysterious physical phenomenon that naturally emerges when the brain reaches a certain level of complexity - as the human brain has. Proponents of artificial intelligence believe modern computers may someday become just as powerful and complex, and, therefore, also exhibit consciousness.

But a growing number of neurologists, psychologists, physicists and philosophers aren't so sure. They wonder if, rather than simply emerging out of physical complexity, consciousness may be something more – something different.

Rather than consciousness emerging out of the physical, perhaps physical reality emerges out of a more fundamental, universal field of consciousness.

A growing number of scientists believe that consciousness may be a fundamental field of awareness outside the brain. Our brains, rather than being the source of consciousness, may simply reflect and interact with it. After decades of exploring various branches of human knowledge, talking with people about their own experiences and considering my own life experience, I believe that, too.

Here's what happened to me. I was obviously familiar with the Christian idea of Jesus being an incarnation of God. As I let go of my traditional

Christian worldview, I still found it interesting that eastern religions viewed all life forms as incarnations of some type of universal consciousness. Buddhism, especially, holds this view, even though it doesn't use the word "God".

Then I discovered that many credible scientists were beginning to view consciousness as more than just something that occurs in the brain. Other credible scientists were beginning to suggest that ultimate reality may be more mental than physical. Some were even suggesting that consciousness actually creates the physical universe.

Suddenly, the idea of one universal field of conscious awareness from which everything emerges made sense. Add to that all the credible PSI and paranormal experiences that traditional science can't explain, and the ideas I'm presenting here, not only make sense, they seem likely.

After more than a decade, there is a mountain of evidence pointing to a universal field of consciousness which allows us to be aware and experience life the way we do. Our awareness and sense of being alive may simply be a local manifestation of that broader universal field of awareness.

The basic question is somewhat like, "Which came first, the chicken or the egg?" Only here, it's, "Which came first and which is more fundamental to reality, the physical or the non-physical?"

What emerges from what? We possess awareness. We are conscious; but where does consciousness reside - in the brain or outside the brain? Is your brain aware of itself, or is some broader universal awareness interacting with your brain in a way that just feels like self-awareness?

Perhaps the perennial philosophy that sees all life forms as individual incarnations of one universal consciousness is pointing toward some yet-to-be-understood truth. As we ponder the possibility of a broader, more fundamental universal consciousness manifesting itself through various physical life forms, here's a crude analogy that may be helpful.

Imagine you are playing a video game in which you control one or more characters. Suppose you become so involved with one character that, for a few moments, you lose yourself in that character. You lose awareness of your "real" self and completely identify with your "virtual" game self.

Go one step further and assume you are controlling multiple characters, and you momentarily lose yourself in all of those characters. In a sense, those characters become a reflection of and a conduit for your own conscious awareness.

I don't recommend it, but you could become so addicted and so engrossed in the game that you actually begin to make various kinds of psychological projection and transference regarding the various characters, and ultimately disassociate from your "real" self. Or, to use a term from quantum physics, become psychologically "entangled" with those various characters. You may even temporarily forget who you really are.

In a similar way, some scientists and philosophers suggest that a universal consciousness is experiencing physical existence and "playing the game of life" through our brains and bodies. It may even become so identified with our bodies and our lives that it temporarily forgets who it really is. It thinks it's you or me when in reality you and I are it. At some point, however, it "wakes up" and realizes it's more than any one individual human being. It's every human being, and actually the source of everything that is.

Eastern mystics would call this "enlightenment" – waking up to who you really are. I know it sounds like science fiction, but keep in mind that many modern scientific truths started out as science fiction.

On a similar note, there are numerous computer scientists who suggest that our universe may be no more than a sophisticated computer simulation or hologram. The question is who or what is observing the simulation?

Others have suggested that reality may be like a dream. The question is who or what is having the dream? There's growing evidence pointing to one universal field of conscious awareness experiencing physical space-time through various life forms such as you and me.

Evidence for One Universal Consciousness

For decades traditional science has assumed that consciousness is nothing more than an emergent property of our brains. It occurs every time a physical brain reaches a certain level of complexity. Some have even gone so far as arguing that consciousness is an illusion.

Actually, claiming that consciousness is an illusion is somewhat of a contradiction because, to have an illusion, there must first be some level of consciousness. Bottom line, the traditional scientific view of consciousness is becoming less and less credible.

Again, a growing number of physicists, neurobiologists and philosophers believe that consciousness may be a fundamental field of awareness outside the brain that our brain simply reflects or interacts with. Many believe that our physical universe may actually materialize out of that non-physical realm of pure awareness. Let's look at some of the growing evidence for this.

Schrodinger's Wave Function

Modern physicists see reality in **particles** and **waves**. In the world of physics, particles occupy particular points in physical space time. They are the building blocks of the physical universe.

Waves, on the other hand, in the context of quantum physics, are mathematical fields of probability and potentiality. They do not actually exist at any particular point in space-time; although they have the potential to "collapse" or "reduce" into a physical particle that does exist at a particular place and time. In a sense waves are like our imagination. They don't physically exist in the way we normally define existence, but they have the potential to.

Without getting too technical, our particular universe appears to be the quantum "reduction" or "collapse" of a wave of potentiality, that physicists call "Schrodinger's wave function". A wave function is a mathematical way of describing this non-physical realm of potentiality or probability that our physical universe seems to "materialize" out of. Erwin Schrodinger was the Austrian physicist who worked out the math.

In a well known physics experiment repeated time and again, a single photon of light is sent through a solid medium containing two slits. The single photon travels through both slits, strikes a wall on the other side and forms a pattern consistent with a wave traveling through two slits. The *single* photon of light is acting like a wave of *multiple* particles.

But as soon as the experimenter attempts to **observe** the photon going through both slits, the photon mysteriously acts like a single particle and goes through just one slit. It then strikes the wall and makes a pattern consistent with a single particle traveling through just one slit. Suddenly, the single photon of light is acting like a single particle.

Here's my point. The only change is the experimenter attempting to consciously **observe** the photon going through the two slits. In other words, prior to conscious observation the photon does not exist in just one particular place, but in every possible place – what physicists call a superposition or a "wave function". In this instance, there are only two possible places or states since there are only two slits to go through. Conscious observation, however, causes it to collapse into one place or one state and travel through only one slit.

Adding to the strangeness, more sophisticated experiments show that conscious observation will also cause a retroactive collapse after the photon has already traveled through the slits, as long as an observation has not yet been made. In other words, conscious observation creates both a particular present reality as well as a corresponding past reality.

On the basis of this and similar experiments, most modern physicists believe that ultimate reality is a non-physical "wave function" of infinite potentiality which has collapsed or is collapsing into one particular physical universe.

In other words, our present world seems to be continually "collapsing" or "emerging" out of a non-physical field of infinite potentiality. Surprisingly, conscious observation seems to trigger the emergence.

This strange but universally accepted phenomenon has caused some physicists to wonder if anything actually exists, in the way we normally define existence, before it is consciously observed.

In other words, does a tree actually fall in the forest if no one is there to observe it fall? Or is both the past and present of a fallen tree created instantaneously when someone enters the forest and begins to observe?

What does this imply about consciousness? Explaining the role of consciousness in quantum collapse or reduction remains a challenge, but it suggests that consciousness is something more than science and medicine have traditionally assumed.

Trying to avoid such implications, some physicists believe the "wave function" is constantly collapsing into every possible reality, creating an infinite number of parallel worlds, independent of conscious observation.

This is called the "many worlds" interpretation, and is popular among some physicists. This interpretation of quantum reduction is bazaar and un-testable, but many scientists accept it in order to avoid the idea of physical reality somehow emerging out of conscious observation.

Other physicists accept the original interpretation that conscious observation causes the collapse. This is called the Copenhagen interpretation. According to this view, our world is the only world that exists and it requires some type of conscious observation to exist. In other words, conscious observation somehow creates physical reality.

A third interpretation initially proposed by physicist John Wheeler builds on the Copenhagen interpretation but adds that our universe did not have a particular past until some type of conscious observation took place. Conscious observation not only creates the present moment, but it also creates a past that leads to the present moment. In other words, the past, present and future are all created somewhat simultaneously, and perhaps moment by moment, by some type of conscious observation.

A fourth interpretation presented by Oxford physicist Roger Penrose, suggests that the non-physical "wave of potentiality" always collapses into physical reality once it reaches a certain level of instability, regardless of whether there is conscious observation or not. Still, even though consciousness does not cause the collapse, consciousness occurs alongside the collapse and becomes part of the fabric of reality, independent of physical brains. In other words, Penrose's theory still holds to a field of conscious awareness outside the physical brain.

Again, what does all this suggest regarding consciousness? It suggests that something like conscious observation exists outside of and prior to the physical universe. Some type of conscious awareness seems to trigger the initial "collapse" of reality from non-physical to physical.

All this suggests a type of panpsychism which sees the entire cosmos as saturated with consciousness. Panpsychism is an old idea that sees the physical universe emerging from a universal field of consciousness. This somewhat ancient philosophical worldview is making a comeback in the world of modern quantum physics. Physicists David Bohm and David Chalmers are other scientists who have recently espoused similar panpsychistic ideas regarding a universal field of consciousness outside the human brain.

Collective Unconscious

A second piece of evidence for a universal field of consciousness is the apparent reality of Carl Jung's "collective unconscious". As already discussed, Jung suggests that if we go deep enough within any individual, we finally arrive at the same place – a place containing all the myths, archetypes and memories of the human race. Again, this "collective unconscious" may be the universal field of consciousness we are contemplating here. Our individual awareness may simply be a reflection of that broader field of universal awareness.

The Illusion of Separateness

A third piece of evidence stems from the modern scientific view that everything is ultimately one thing. We experience reality in different places at different times and in different forms; but most of the separateness seems to be an illusion. Quantum concepts such as **non-locality** and **entanglement** suggest that all physical reality is one eternal continuum, within which all information is available instantaneously across the entire continuum regardless of physical distance.

To the dismay of many traditional physicists, this modern discovery violates the traditional assumption that our universe is only four dimensional, and that nothing can travel across it faster than the speed of light, including information. There seems to be a higher dimension of reality transcending our everyday four dimensional reality. Einstein initially rejected this new idea of higher dimensions as "spooky action at a distance".

Traditional scientific and philosophical questions such as "What existed before the big bang?" or "Why do we all experience the same reality at the same time" find possible answers in this idea of one universal field of consciousness transcending four dimensional space-time. Our ability to know and interact with each other as we do may stem from this single shared field of awareness.

PSI

Scientific research related to psychic phenomena (PSI) provides more evidence for a non-physical universal consciousness at the heart of reality. Pre-cognition, out of body experiences, past life regression during hypnosis and mind reading can potentially be explained by a field of universal awareness saturating and connecting everything.

Once at a computer conference, I knew a few seconds before a drawing that my number would be drawn. It was insignificant and unimportant, but still a clear example of knowing something I should not have been able to know.

I personally know a couple near Dallas, Tx. who met with a well known, but now deceased, psychic, Jeffe Murphy, who also worked with local police to help solve crimes. She told them specific things that would occur in their future that were impossible for her to know. Over the next several months, life saving events occurred exactly as predicted. Again, one explanation is the existence of a universal field of knowledge which is occasionally accessible to some individuals.

On a less sensational level, the unusually deep love and empathy we sometimes feel for certain people may also suggest a deep oneness at a subconscious level. Love at first is one example. Meeting someone for the first time and feeling that you've known them forever is another. I had this experience with my wife. We were married 3 months after we met and have remained together as best friends for over 40 years and counting.

From a historical perspective, ideas occurring in separate parts of the ancient world at almost the same time may point to a shared universal consciousness. Monotheism, laws such as Hammurabi's code and the 10 commandments, as well as the similar intellectual advancements reflected in the teachings of Buddha, Jesus, Plato, Lao Tzu and others all suggest connections that go beyond traditional evolution.

Out of body experiences provide more evidence for consciousness residing outside the brain. While many can be explained using traditional medical and psychological models, some clearly cannot.

There are credible accounts of people in accidents and on battlefields who observed themselves from outside their bodies and later described the details in ways that defy explanation. This obviously points to the possibility of individual consciousness residing outside the brain, but it may also point to one universal consciousness that we all share.

Dreams, which are still somewhat of a neurological mystery, also point to expanded levels of consciousness that transcend time and space. Abraham Lincoln dreamed about his assassination weeks before it occurred. Perhaps we occasionally access a universal field of shared awareness during our dreams.

During my years as a minister, I had several PSI experiences that I still cannot fully explain using traditional science. As a minister, I experienced rare moments of pre-cognition during prayer. On a couple of occasions, I clearly felt a strong force when touching another person.

I have had a near death experience in which I felt an unexpected and overwhelming sense of clarity and peace.

Again, these experiences suggest to me that consciousness is more than just an emergent phenomenon of highly complex physical brains. There seems to be a universal field of consciousness saturating everything and causing connections and insights that defy traditional explanations.

In a more recent period of meditation, I seemed to have transcended my small sense of self and experienced a deep oneness with the universe. Such experiences are hard to describe, and I hesitate to share them because of how easily and often such experiences turn out to be illusions. But even if many are, others seem to suggest a broader realm of conscious awareness that transcends our individuality.

Thin Places

Similar to PSI phenomena, consider the numerous claims related to "near death" and "shared death" experiences. Dr. Raymond Moody describes numerous individuals who had out of body experiences while a loved one was dying. They claim to have briefly glimpsed a realm beyond death along with the dying person.

Also consider the thousands who claim to have encountered deceased loved ones, either directly or through mediums. While most are subsequently proven to be fraudulent, there are credible examples that defy traditional explanation.

Ancient Celtic spirituality used the term "thin places" to describe occasions when the lines between life and death became fuzzy. I personally know a few whom I believe had credible encounters with loved ones who had died.

As I stated earlier, the resurrection of Jesus could have been such an experience involving one or two of his closest followers - perhaps Mary Magdalene, to whom he seems to have had a special bond. Again, events like this obviously point to the possibility of individual consciousness existing outside the brain, but they may also point to one universal consciousness saturating everything.

Forever Family Foundation[9] is a non-profit organization that explores claims regarding the afterlife. They also examine "mediums" in an attempt to weed out those who are fraudulent. Only a small percentage of mediums pass their stringent certification process which is offered free of charge.

The primary focus of Forever Family Foundation is to help grieving individuals and families deal with the loss of a loved one. They do so from a scientific rather than a religious perspective. Organizations like FFF should have a voice in our continuing exploration of death.

While some of the above examples do not necessarily point to one universal consciousness, they do suggest other possibilities that may help us face the grief and fear that death entails. They certainly raise the possibility that life on earth is far more than we currently understand.

Reincarnation

Phenomena that some psychiatrists interpret as evidence for reincarnation may also point to the idea of one universal consciousness. A belief in some type of reincarnation has been part of numerous cultures – if not most – from time immemorial.

Universal ideas related to reincarnation may simply be another mechanism to soften the pain of death; but they might also stem from a deep universal intuition that our normal experience of self is incomplete.

It's easy to imagine a universal consciousness manifesting itself in various individuals. It's also easy to imagine various groups of individual manifestations that are closely connected or "entangled" in some way – perhaps through ancestral lineage, environment, culture or some unique combination of DNA.

---

[9] https://forever-family-foundation.herokuapp.com/

The individual "selves" in these groups may experience a higher than average degree of shared consciousness. During their lifetimes, they may occasionally share memories or awareness. This experience might feel like individual reincarnation. In some ways, it is; but it's also more evidence that we all share one universal field of awareness.

Mystical Experiences

Obviously, there is a common thread running through all religious traditions that posits a universal consciousness from which the physical world emanates. Most call it "God", although "God" is often defined in radically different ways by each tradition.

The more mystical elements within religion often describe a pan**en**theistic[10] "God" which is similar to the universal consciousness I have been referring to. There seems to be something deep within the human psyche that is often drawn toward such an understanding of reality.

Several years ago, while living in an old duplex near the ocean in Daytona Beach, Florida, I experienced one of those rare but "meaningful coincidences" that Carl Jung's discusses in his writings on synchronicity.

I was awake most the night, reviewing my life and trying to make sense of it. It was only the second or third time in my entire life I remember doing that. It was somewhat of a "dark night of the soul" during which time I was searching for a sense of meaning and purpose.

The sun finally came up after a long night of remembering and thinking. I had long given up on traditional religion, but for some unknown reason, I picked up a prayer book I had not read in quite a while. I turned to the scripture readings for that particular summer day. I was shocked, but also comforted, when I began to read from Psalm 119:48 "I stay awake through the night, thinking about your promise."

---

[10] Pantheism equates all reality with God. In contrast, pan**en**theism sees God as saturating all reality and also transcending it.

I know this can easily be explained as a meaningless coincidence, but for me it was more. What are the odds of me staying awake on that particular night, pondering those particular questions, and then reading those particular words in that particular book on that particular morning? Highly improbable to say the least.

I have experienced "coincidences" like that on several occasions. There was no great revelation of truth involved. My questions were not answered. But I felt I was part of something much bigger than myself.

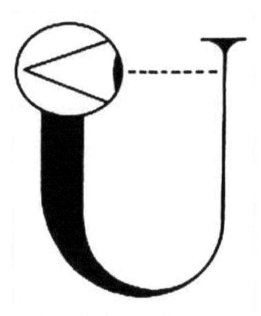

John Wheeler's illustration of a participatory universe in which the universe observes itself through human consciousness.[11]

---

[11] John Wheeler, Beyond Black Holes, 1979

Who Are You?

"And you? When will you begin that long journey into yourself?" Rumi

Regarding freedom from the fear of death, how can the above speculations help us realize that freedom? Beyond the expanded sense of self we discussed earlier, ideas of a universally shared field of conscious awareness offer even more possibilities.

It is not irrational nor is it simply what psychiatrists call "magical thinking" to believe that some type of universal consciousness is at the heart of reality. Nor is it irrational or unscientific to believe that our personal sense of consciousness and this broader universal consciousness may actually be the same thing. In that very possible scenario, each of us may be a localized instance, manifestation or incarnation of that one universal consciousness.

Obviously, this is good news regarding death. Because, while your body will die, the real you, which is this universal consciousness, never will. Universal consciousness is eternal.

Obviously, at this point, we must be very careful to avoid the "slippery slope" leading back into religion. There is some value in religious language and religious symbolism as long as we don't take things too literally. Like science fiction and poetry, religion can sometimes communicate ideas that are helpful.

Of course, we must avoid religious dogmas such as divine revelation, systems of reward and punishment, authority based on scriptures or ordinations, literalistic and dualistic thinking and calls for worship.

"Spiritual" may be a better word than "religion", but it too can be problematic. Words like "paranormal" and "metaphysical" are sometimes used, but they, too, raise flags for many who equate them with pseudoscience. Whatever words we use, we must allow them to simply point to a place where words can't go.

As we discussed in the chapter related to Jesus, there are many ancient and modern philosophies that point to something like a universal consciousness manifesting itself in various life forms. Some are less religious than others.

In Taoism there is no omnipotent being who created and controls the universe. The universe emerges from and flows with the Tao. The Tao is not "God", nor is it worshipped by Taoists. Physicist Fritjof Capra's 1975 book, The Tao of Physics, does an excellent job comparing ancient Taoist thought to modern quantum physics. One can draw numerous parallels between the Tao and the modern concept of a universal field of conscious awareness from which everything emerges.

Buddha avoided the idea of "God" because he believed the concept was unnecessary, was not supported by evidence and was usually rooted in fear. Not all, but many Buddhists are atheists or agnostics. Buddhism uses the non-personal term, nirvana, to describe a universal state of pure consciousness beyond all physical manifestations.

As already explored, the teachings of Jesus can easily be interpreted in ways that point to one universal consciousness that we are all "incarnations" of. Beyond the teachings of Jesus, other voices in early Christianity seem to reflect a similar idea.

The early Christian missionary, Paul of Tarsus, wrote, "we, who are many, are one body in Christ…it is not I who live, but Christ lives through me…Christ is everything and he is in everything." Paul seemed to distinguish between the man Jesus and the "Christ" - "Christ" referring not to the man Jesus, but to one universal consciousness indwelling each of us. Jesus, like Buddha, simply realized his "Christ" nature more than most.

The early Christian doctrine of theosis contains a similar idea and is still part of Eastern Orthodox Christianity. The ancient Christian phrase, "God became human so that humans could become God", summarizes the idea of theosis and suggests a much broader concept of God than that presented by western Christianity.

Luke, another Biblical writer, describes "God" as the one "in whom we live, move and have our being." The Biblical writer, John, who often describes a more eastern or Buddhist Jesus, also broadens the concept of God by stating bluntly, "God is love. Those who love know God. Those who do not love, do not know God." Again, while Christianity quickly became more Roman, Platonic and dualistic in its theology, eastern ideas of one universal consciousness are clearly seen in its earliest writings.

The 13th century Islamic mystic and poet, Rumi, suggested a similar idea when he wrote, "Everything in the universe is within you."

Some may want to name this universal consciousness, "God"; but the word "God" carries a lot of unhealthy religious baggage. Traditional images of God separate God from the physical universe, and from you and me. That's a mistake, because everything is ultimately one thing. This one thing is always changing and manifesting itself in an infinite variety of ways, but it's still just one essence. And if our bodies could perceive the cosmos in 4 spatial dimensions instead of just 3, we would see that it's also just one moment – one eternal now.

In traditional religion, "God" doesn't feel our pain directly through our bodies, he only "hears" our painful cries and responds because he cares about us. This may sound comforting, but it creates an unscientific and unhealthy dualism that is the basis for most religion. It imagines a creator separate from its creation.

Not only is there little evidence for this, but this dualistic thinking lies at the heart of the judgmental divisiveness that makes religion so dangerous. It leads to other dualistic concepts such as secular and sacred, clergy and laity, worthy and unworthy, heaven and hell, etc. It allows us to easily exclude people who don't look or think like us and ignore places and things we do not consider "sacred". It allows us to ignore the oneness that connects everything.

Based on the best science, everything is ultimately one thing. It is eternal and ever changing. It transcends time and space. At its core, it's non-physical and may be conscious. Our consciousness may simply be a reflection of that one universal consciousness. Our small sense of "self" is somewhat of an illusion. Our real "self" may actually be this one larger universal "self". You and I may simply be physical localizations of that one universal consciousness.

When Albert Einstein presented his theory of general relativity to the world, people were stunned because the theory presented a revolutionary view of reality completely at odds with every day perceptions. His ideas turned conventional Newtonian physics upside down. Newton's scientific laws still worked in many practical ways, but Einstein's theories revealed their flaws and ultimate incompleteness.

Einstein's theories ultimately led to quantum physics which is even more bazaar. As physicist Niels Bohr stated, "Anyone who is not shocked by quantum theory has not understood it." And as physicist, Richard Feynman quipped, "If you think you understand quantum mechanics, you don't."

Ideas regarding a universal consciousness experiencing physical existence through us may also seem strange and bazaar to most people, especially those living in the Western hemisphere – but perhaps no more than general relativity, higher dimensions, parallel universes, non-locality, quantum entanglement and Schrodinger's wave function.

Call it what you want, Universal Consciousness, Collective Unconscious, Higher Self, Higher Power, Mother Nature, Tao, Universal Wave Function; or do what some ancient Jews did and refuse to call it anything. Whatever you call it, it may be the only thing there is, and to paraphrase Buddha, "You may be that."

Humans have long searched for "God". Religion exploits that search. Actually, searching for "God" may be like a fish swimming through the ocean searching for the ocean. The eye cannot see itself because it is the eye. It can only see itself reflected in something else. For those who are searching for "God" or whatever the word "God" points to, perhaps they are that which they are searching for.

Some of the rather provocative ideas suggested above are obviously speculative, but they are also based on credible science and avoid the pitfalls of religion. Returning to the main purpose of this rather long section, they also give us new ways to think about death and free ourselves from the anxiety and fear that death produces.

Individuality

This somewhat speculative, yet intriguing idea that each of us may be an individual incarnation of one universal consciousness raises several new questions regarding our individuality. Even if our larger self never dies, what happens to our smaller, individual self?

At death, does our small individual self merge with other small individual selves that have already died, into one larger self? Are we like individual waves dissolving back into the one ocean from which they arose?

As our individual self merges back into one universal consciousness, do we remember this life? Do we suddenly "remember" all other individual lives in the same way? If you and I share the same universal consciousness, why aren't we conscious of each other's mental thoughts and feelings right now?

Let's think more about what it means to be an individual self. As stated earlier, modern science suggests there is no actual self. It seems to be an illusion, as Buddha taught many centuries ago. The self cannot be located in the brain and it certainly changes dramatically over time.

You are a completely different "self" right now, than you were as a baby or a child or a teenager or a young adult. There's a connecting thread, but, basically, I'm no longer the middle aged "self" I was a decade or so ago. Even the physical cells that comprise our brain and body are all replaced every seven years or so.

Beyond the fact that the self is always changing, there is also the question of what comprises the self. You tend to see yourself as more than just your body; but place yourself in a very different body, and you will become a very different self over time.

Far more significant than your body are your memories. Place different memories in your body and you will obviously be an entirely different self. The significance of memory becomes painfully obvious in people with dementia or Alzheimer's. More than anything else, your sense of self seems to be, primarily, a collection of memories.

It seems that beyond your physical brain's continual processing, storing and recalling of memories, there is no real self to survive physical death. Your self is somewhat like a rainbow which only appears when a particular configuration of sunlight, moisture and air is observed by the human eye. Similarly, your sense of self only appears when a particular configuration of memories is observed by some type of conscious awareness.

Another example is the Big Dipper, which only appears as you become conscious of particular memories in the context of a particular collection of stars. Again, your sense of self only manifests itself as you become conscious of particular memories in the context of a particular lifespan.

The fact that "self" is so fragile and fleeting is why enlightened teachers like Jesus and Buddha encouraged us to "die to self" or "detach from self". Perhaps we worry too much about individual survival of death. Perhaps we are thinking too small.

Lower and Higher Dimensions

An understanding of dimensions is crucial to understanding the physics of reality…and possibly the nature of the individual self. Take the time to grasp the ideas that follow because they will open up intriguing new possibilities for understanding who you are.

To exist in one dimension is to be a line.

_____

To exist in two dimensions is to be a portrait. You possess height and width, but no depth.

To exist in three dimensions is to be a statue. You possess height, width and depth, but no change or movement.

Now, if we add the dimension of time, the statue can change and move from past to future like you and I do. Life, as we know it, seems to require at least three spatial dimensions, plus the dimension of time.

Below is an attempt to add a fourth spatial dimension to the three dimensional cube above.

But before we try to imagine existing in more dimensions, let's imagine existing in fewer dimensions. If you were just two dimensional, you would be like a flat picture. Add the dimension of time and you would be like a moving picture or video – changing position moment by moment. Pause here for a moment and imagine life in "Flat Land".[12] You exist in a portrait that allows movement.

Keep in mind you would not be able to see the picture from outside the picture like you do in three dimensions. There is no space outside the picture. So when you look at someone else in the picture, all you see is their edge facing you. It would be like looking at the edge of a puzzle piece rather than seeing the entire puzzle piece from outside the puzzle.

Also, you could not pass by other pieces of the picture because there is no space outside the picture allowing you to pass. You could only pass something by going over or under it. This is life in a two dimensional world, plus a third dimension of time allowing movement.

Before we leave "Flat Land", imagine a three dimensional person

---

[12] A two dimensional world described in the book, Flatland, by Edwin A. Abbott, 1992.

passing through your two dimensional world. It would be like you passing through a portrait. What would you look like to the people in the portrait? As they watch a three dimensional person passing through their two dimensional portrait, they would only see thin slices of the edge of the person as the person passes through the flat plane of the picture.

Again, it would be like seeing only the edges of the puzzle piece, because people in the portrait cannot step outside the picture and see the whole picture at once. They could not see the entire you – just slices of you moment by moment.

Here's another illustration that may be helpful. Allow the page you are reading now to represent Flatland. Place the tips of your fingers and thumb against the page.

Now imagine what the tips of your fingers and thumb would look like to a two dimensional creature in Flatland. They would only see the edges of your fingers and thumb that are actually touching the page. They would actually see five separate entities because the hand that connects the fingers is in a third dimension outside the page, which they cannot see. In other words, what is actually one thing in three dimensions appears to be five separate things in two dimensions.

The point is that adding dimensions allows you to see more of reality. Adding dimensions allows your conscious awareness to expand. **Things which appear to be separated in a lower dimension may be part of a single whole in a higher dimension.** Each of us, while separated in four dimensions, may actually be connected in a higher dimension.

Keep in mind that our brain is only three dimensional, which means it can see three dimensional space all at once; but it can only experience the fourth dimension of time moment by moment. We can understand the fourth dimension of time, but we can only experience it moment by moment. Memory allows us to connect these moments chronologically and create a sense of self, existing through time.

But what if our brain was four dimensional and could see four-dimensional space-time all at once? We could see all the moments of our life all at once. We would no longer need memory.

Perhaps something like this happens when a person having a near death experience claims their whole life flashed before their eyes. It's almost as though their conscious awareness was no longer limited by their three dimensional brain and they saw their entire life in four dimensions.

In that scenario, "self" is no longer a collection of memories; rather, it's simply the observation of a particular block of space-time, all at once. Although we normally don't experience reality in that way, we can imagine it.

Modern physics suggests there are possibly 10 or 11 dimensions comprising reality. Slow down, stretch and exercise your brain here for a moment. Imagine another type of "memory" or "expanded consciousness" which allows us to connect various blocks of space time in a way that creates a "super self" consisting of multiple individual lives.

In other words, instead of being conscious of just your own life moment by moment; you are conscious of various lives, individual by individual. Could this be what universal consciousness experiences as it experiences the consciousnesses of multiple individuals, but still differentiates between them in the same way that we differentiate between different memories of different moments?

Of course, we could keep adding dimensions until a universal consciousness experiences everything imaginable simultaneously. Again, the possibility of 10 or more dimensions, which is how reality may actually be, adds numerous new and radical possibilities as to how we might view consciousness and the individual self.

Regarding death, it could be that the various dimensions of reality allow our lives to exist forever in a universal field of conscious awareness. The only caveat is that, while a much expanded consciousness continues, your current life associated with your current body does end.

But, keep in mind this is similar to your infant body or your teenage body or your younger adult body also ending as you grow older. Even your current small self is larger than your ever changing body.

And just as your sense of self keeps expanding as you experience additional stages of life, perhaps your sense of self will expand even more, as you become conscious of a broader existence in a higher dimension beyond your current block of space-time. This may happen at death as consciousness breaks free from the limitations of your current physical brain and your current four dimensional world.

Here is one final intriguing possibility that sounds like science fiction but has some basis in modern physics as well as human experience. What if, at death, our consciousness doesn't expand to all dimensions of reality; but rather expands to just 5 or 6? This might allow you to become conscious of multiple lives, but not all lives. Perhaps you become conscious of your whole family tree, or some other particular group of lives. There is some evidence for this in recent experiments with past life regression under hypnosis.

Various dimensions of reality seem to allow universal consciousness to be one and many at the same time. This supports the idea that while the self we think we are is actually one universal consciousness, there is also a level of individuality that is distinct from it. The Christian concept of the Trinity, in which Jesus is both God and man at the same time, points to a similar idea.

Conclusion

The main point here is that the existence of one universal consciousness manifesting itself in multiple dimensions radically changes our view of death. Death is no longer the loss of anything. It may be the end of a particular bodily experience, but it may also be the expansion of a much broader conscious experience.

I'm again reminded of Buddha's and Jesus' admonition that we not worry excessively about the loss of our earthly lives. There will be more and better, not less or worse. Our small self dies, but a larger self continues.

How we remember our small self remains somewhat of a mystery, but perhaps not that different from how we remember our infant self or child self from years ago. Memories are wonderful but all memories fade over time. Perhaps we should focus less on the past and more on the future. Perhaps we should focus less on our small self and more on our larger self.

As Americans, we focus on the individual more than most because of what historians call our "rugged individualism". Other cultures not so much. Even the way we name ourselves reveals a distinction between eastern and western attitudes toward the individual. In the western hemisphere, individual names come before family names, placing the emphasis on the individual. In the eastern hemisphere, the family name comes before the individual name, placing the emphasis on the larger family.

Years ago I worked with a dear friend, Nyit-Wah Yong. As a typical American, I always addressed her as Nyit or Nyit-Wah. She informed me one day that if I were to address her that way in front of her family, they would not know who I was referring to. All her sibling's names began with Nyit-Wah. It was her last name, Yong, which differentiated her from her siblings.

This is a subtle but significant difference that reflects different cultural attitudes toward the individual self. Buddha and Jesus were obviously more eastern than western. In contrast, American religion and culture is far more individualized. This may make it more difficult for Americans to let go of the small self and focus on a larger self in the ways I'm suggesting here.

Why Are We Here?

We are considering the possibility of one universal consciousness from which everything emanates. If true, it obviously raises interesting and perhaps comforting possibilities related to death and a possible afterlife. It also raises other questions as to why we are here and why the universe is the way it is.

Why is our consciousness now limited to only four dimensions? Why are we, at least temporarily, trapped in a smaller individualized "self" and cut off from a broader conscious awareness?

Also, why are we aware of this particular moment rather than some other moment? The fact that we are all aware of this particular moment together strongly suggests a higher awareness that connects us all. Still, why this moment?

Moreover, why does our awareness of particular moments flow in a particular direction – from past to future? There is some yet-to-be-understood relationship between conscious awareness, the present moment and the flow of time. For some reason the universal wave of potentiality we described earlier is collapsing at a particular point and in a particular direction.

The universe is obviously evolving and we are both observing and participating in that evolution. Perhaps a universal field of awareness is evolving toward a particular future state of being – what some have called an "omega point"?[13]

While history involves a lot of "two steps forward, one step back", we do seem to be making some progress in our global pursuit of happiness – granted the process is painfully slow. Humans appear to be slightly more civilized than 500 years ago. More and more people seem to be realizing that "we all do better when we all do better".

Even if our species destroys itself, perhaps another species will learn from our failures and finally achieve a higher state of wellbeing that history seems to cry out for. There may be value in occasionally being reminded that humans may not be as central to existence as our egos like to imagine.

Such a final state does not necessarily require a universal field of awareness that is intelligent. The same seemingly blind processes that now drive evolution could produce such a final state of well being. The

---

[13] Term coined by scientist and Jesuit priest, Pierre Teilhard de Chardin, describing a future state of the universe toward which everything is being drawn.

natural pursuit of pleasure and resistance to pain that all conscious life forms seem to possess could be driving us in that direction. A universal consciousness would experience that final state whether it designed it or not.

Alternatively, some scientists believe that the universe already is everything that it ever was or ever will be. As suggested earlier, the past, present and future may exist already and simultaneously; despite the fact that we only experience them one moment at a time. If the future does already exist, as Einstein's theories seem to suggest, perhaps the universe is reviewing or re-living its own history through us.

According to this view, the future has already happened – we just haven't experienced it yet. To use a movie analogy, it's like watching a movie for the first time and not knowing the ending, even though the entire movie obviously already exists from beginning to end.

This also raises questions related to free will. It could be that a particular final state of the universe is pre-determined, but how the universe gets there and how long it takes is open ended. Perhaps individual life forms have a limited degree of free will that helps determine which particular path the universe takes.

On the other hand, perhaps the universe has no purpose or grand scheme in the traditional sense. Perhaps our universe is simply the means by which some higher field of awareness experiences physical existence. Perhaps we are its ears, mouth, nose, eyes, skin, thoughts and emotions.

It experiences the universe through us, both the pleasure and the pain. It may or may not possess its own self-awareness and intelligence. It may only experience self-awareness and intelligence through us.

Most of us need a sense of purpose. We seem to be driven to accomplish things. Some philosophers suggest that we resist this "will" to accomplish and just enjoy the moment. Others remind us of how boring and irresponsible such a life might be. We are often at our best and happiest when meeting a challenge. Regardless of what the future holds long term, we can still enjoy a sense of purpose as we engage the day to day challenges of life.

Bottom line: there's no way to know if the universe we inhabit is moving toward a predetermined future or is simply going with the flow. Some see life on earth as a school or boot camp preparing for some future age. Others see it as an amusement park to simply be enjoyed. Speculations are endless. Freely explore the possibilities and enjoy the ride.

Somewhere Over the Rainbow

At times, I feel there is some kind of higher purpose. Occasionally, we seem to get lucky in ways that almost seem more than luck – meaningful coincidences, synchronicity. Occasionally, a faint voice softly whispers, "You are not alone." Sometimes, we may even hear something as radical and unexplainable as, "I know you and I love you."

Avoid religion, but don't be afraid to explore a philosophy, or even a spirituality, that sees the universe as a friendly and meaningful place. Don't completely close your mind to the possibility that "Somewhere over the rainbow, dreams you dare to dream really do come true."

Maybe, rather than a sophisticated computer simulation, life is a dream; and death is simply waking up. The nursery rhyme "Row Row Your Boat" was actually written to express such an idea. Perhaps dreams of a "heavenly" existence, bathed in love, without pain and death, are more than just dreams. Who knows?

Similar to how the quantum wave function represents every possible location of one physical particle, perhaps our universe is a wave function representing every possible incarnation of one universal consciousness. When the wave has fully collapsed, perhaps there will be just one "perfect" multi-dimensional incarnation that we are all part of. Perhaps evolution is the path to that.

Someone wrote,

"Please don't tell the bumble bee
That he is not able to fly;
Lest he like us,
Fall from the sky."

We know so little - so, so little. Here's why. Through our 5 senses of sight, smell, touch, taste and sound, we directly experience only a very small fraction of reality. Some species experience more than that. For example bees can sense ultraviolet light. Dogs can hear higher sound frequencies than humans. Homing pigeons can sense magnetic waves. Some fish can sense electromagnetic waves. Humans experience an extremely small portion of what comprises the physical world.

But that's not all. Much of what we sense is immediately filtered out of our conscious awareness so that we are not overwhelmed by all the information available to our 5 senses. We tend to focus on what matters at the time.

But that's not all. The small amount of data that survives this initial filtering process is then transferred to various areas in our brains via neurons, at which time other parts of our brain create a mental representation using the raw data that makes it from our physical senses to our brain. Our brains will even "make up" data if needed in order to make the image consistent with past mental images.

You can begin to see why it's important to distinguish between reality and our own mental representation of reality. They are very different.

But that's not all. The mental representation we create based on the limited amount of information our 5 senses send to our brain, is then saved as memories. Much of the mental representation is lost, in that our memories are selective and also fade over time.

But that's not all. We then use these highly filtered and often faded memories to form ideas and opinions which determine our overall world view.

But that's not all. Our particular world view then begins to further limit the type of future information that makes it from our 5 senses to our brain. This subtle and gradual "brainwashing" is what creates cultural diversity as well as individual biases and blind spots.

With all this in mind, it should not surprise us that our world is so conflicted regarding so many things. It should also keep us humble regarding our own ideas and more open to new ideas. As my dad used to remind me, the smartest people will always know how little they know.

But along with a healthy demand for humility regarding the big questions in life, there is also hope in what we don't know. Those who insist that this physical world is all there is are probably wrong. Death may not be the end game that so many fear.

"Oh Death, Where Is Thy Sting?"

One universal consciousness at the foundation of existence opens the door to infinite possibilities related to life and death. As I said earlier, science is the best path to discovering truth. Modern science, especially in the areas of quantum physics and neurobiology, are radically changing our traditional views of reality; shedding new light on old ideas and bringing new ideas to light.

As I stated earlier, I believe there is a universal field of awareness which allows us to be aware and experience life the way we do. Our awareness is that awareness. When I die, that awareness continues.

Do my memories continue, also? I'm not sure. But the awareness that allows me to know and connect to the world around me does continue. In that very real sense, I continue also.

For me, this seems to be a healthy and credible way to understand human consciousness and physical death. This particular worldview answers the fundamental questions of life and death better than any other that I am aware of. These ideas can be both enlightening and comforting. It draws from common threads of truth running through numerous scientific, philosophical, mystical and religious approaches to life.

To say it in a more traditional way, I believe we are all various manifestations of one universal field of conscious awareness. There are times when we may intuitively know what we always have been and always will be. When we glimpse that deeper essence, all is good. Nothing can separate us from it or destroy it. We are that.

All of the above can lessen our fear of death. Christians make a big deal about the cross upon which Jesus was crucified. They selfishly turn it into a symbol of judgment and punishment.

The Biblical message of Jesus' cross is much more positive and hopeful. Jesus looked into the heavens and asked, "Why have you forsaken me?" Why is life so painful? Why am I dying?

But then he remembered his own words and possibly the words of Buddha. "Truly, truly, I say to you, unless a grain of wheat falls into the earth and dies, it remains alone; but if it dies, it bears much fruit...Whoever wishes to save his life will lose it, but whoever loses his life will save it."

He then looked deep within and said to the cosmos, "Into thy hands I commit my spirit." I trust that which always was and always will be – that which all of us ultimately are.

A Dream

On October 19th and 20th, 1916, I had a several vivid dreams – so vivid I wrote them down. I don't always remember my dreams, but these were different.

On the first night, I dreamed I was crying because of so many people in my life and elsewhere who had died. It seemed to last for hours.

On the second night I dreamed there was a water leak in the apartment I was in. It was threatening adjacent apartments as well as mine. There were lots of well meaning people trying to help, but they were of little help. I felt frustrated and knew that I had to resolve the problem myself.

Later that same night, I dreamed there was small handicapped female child hugging me and loving me. We were on the 2nd floor of a structure that was collapsing. The child was in my arms, and I was trying to get her to the ground. Bad people were attacking us from below. There seemed to be no way out.

Suddenly a large black female panther with pink lines on her back, which almost looked like small wings, appeared and ran off the bad guys. The panther gently rode us to the ground. I woke up.

I thought about the dreams over the next few days during times of meditation. It finally became very clear to me that I am the dying people and the one crying. I am the useless ones with good intentions and the one having to resolve things on my own. I am the little girl, the one holding the little girl, the bad people, and the black panther.

We all are.

In other words, we are more than the small, individual self we have become so addicted to. The death of that small self is not the tragedy so many imagine. The more we know, the less there is to fear. Open yourself to all the possibilities of existence. Don't be afraid - be free.

Who Are We?

We are 10 billion waves,
But we are also the ocean.
We are a trillion rays of light,
But we are also the sun.
We are many particular things,
But we are also one thing.
We are right here, right now,
But we are also everywhere and always.

We are many songs,
But one singer.
We are many poems,
But one poet.
We are many paintings,
But one artist.
We are many thoughts,
But one thinker.
We are many emotions,
But one heart.
We are many moons,
But one sun.

John Alan Shope

Freedom to Enjoy Life Responsibly

"I know there is strength in the differences between us. I know there is comfort, where we overlap." Ani DiFranco

I started to call this section "Freedom to Love". But the word "love" is a lot like the word "God". It's vague, loaded with emotion and can mean many different things to different people.

The Greeks had several different words for love. There was sexual love, brotherly love, parental love and a less selfish, unconditional love. We just have the one word which makes it more difficult to use.

For many, love is freedom from hate - both hatred of self and hatred of others. We're often told that to love deeply, one must feel loved and love oneself. That's probably true.

Others have suggested that the main reason we are here on planet Earth is to learn to love. Not a bad idea to live by.

Still, I decided to use the phrase, "Free to Enjoy Life Responsibly" because it strikes a good balance between taking care of yourself and respecting others. It reminds me of something my seminary professor used to say. "You have the right to stick your fist out anytime, anywhere - as long as someone else's face isn't already there."

You often see the phrase "Enjoy Responsibly" on a bottle of beer. It reminds the customer to enjoy the alcohol; but don't become addicted and don't hurt other people – in public, on the road or at home. That's a good motto to live by, also.

It actually summarizes much of what we've said about freedom. Life is short, enjoy it. Be here now. Wear life like a loose jacket. Live, laugh and love.

Don't let others exploit you with religious or political propaganda. As Bob Dylan once said, "Don't be a pawn in their game." I'm reminded of Paul Simon's song, "50 Ways to Leave Your Lover." There's more than 50 ways to leave all the people and systems that exploit you. "Get yourself free." Do the research, look at all the data and think for yourself. Step back and try to see the bigger picture.

Beyond not letting others exploit you, don't exploit yourself. Know when to say when. When you feel yourself becoming too attached to a particular pleasure, learn to let go for awhile. You'll never have enough money or enough clothes, enough sex, a big enough house or enough pleasure of any kind.

Enjoy the stuff that sends a flood of endorphins through your brain, but also enjoy the mental stillness and moments of nothingness that feel just a blissful. Learn to be still and breathe for long periods of time.

Get free and stay free from all the demons within that want to enslave you. Keep things simple and low maintenance. Travel light. Learn to let go of the past and live in the present. Plan for the future but don't become obsessed and worry yourself to an early grave.

Finally, Don't exploit others. We really are all connected. Everything really is just one thing. You may not think so right now, but, we all do better when we all do better. You feel the effect of other people's pain. What goes around comes around.

As John Donne wrote in "For Whom the Bell Tolls", "No man is an island entire of itself…if a clod be washed away by the sea, Europe is the less…any man's death diminishes me, because I am involved in mankind; therefore never send to know for whom the bell tolls; it tolls for thee."

At some deep level, I am you and you are me. Walk a mile in my shoes.

The more you get to know me, the more you will discover pieces of yourself in me. We all live in a delicate ecosystem which will preserve itself at all cost – even if it means sacrificing the human species.

Don't enjoy life at someone else's expense – even if that someone else is an unknown face on the other side of the world. They hurt for their children just as you hurt for yours. Be still and feel their pain.

The inability to feel empathy for other people is a common component in several mental illnesses. Don't selfishly neglect other people. Don't be so quick to write off the poor as lazy and irresponsible. "There but by the grace of God go you." Don't be that person who was born on third base and thought they hit a triple.

I'm not saying we should all be like Jesus or St. Francis or Mother Theresa – giving away all our possessions and living in solidarity with the poor and homeless. It would no doubt be an enlightening experience and teach us a lot about happiness; but that's not who we are, at least not yet.

I am saying see other people as different versions of you. Look around at anyone. If you were born into their family, with their genes, raised in their environment, had the same random things happen to you that happened to them – you would be just like them. They are simply that version of you. Be merciful to that version of you – and the other 8 billion versions of you scattered across the globe.

This is a fairly accurate statistic. Half the world is worrying about what they will eat tomorrow. Half the world is not. Which half were you born into? Don't neglect those who were born into the other half, by no choice of their own. Enjoy the ride, but don't forget there are others in the car and on the highway.

Many are quick to remind us that we can't just keep giving hungry people fish. We must teach hungry people how to fish. True, but, we must also make sure they have reliable fishing poles, sufficient bait and access to a pond with fish in it.

Again, I'm not saying save the world. I'm not even saying save your community. I am saying don't be part of the problem. Don't be complicit in an unjust system that keeps exploiting the weak and powerless.

In a nutshell: laugh responsibly, live simply and, occasionally, be willing to love sacrificially.

Oneness

In the previous section we discussed the evidence for and the implications of one universal consciousness experiencing physical existence through each of us. If we are all various manifestations of that one universal consciousness, then, in a sense, we are all different versions of each other.

As Buddha taught, "You are that." Or as the eastern greeting, "namaste", translates, "the divine in me acknowledges the divine in you."

The oneness we all share is the basis for love. Love and kindness are a natural result of the oneness we share with all living things. If you and I share the same essence, we really are brothers and sisters. Other people are our family. The planet is our family. It would be irrational for you to hurt your family. When you hurt me or neglect me, you are separating yourself from me in a way that is unnatural and blind to the web of being that connects us all.

Does that mean we stop defending ourselves from viruses, aggressive animals or blind and broken humans? No. Does that mean we all become vegetarians? Not necessarily. Does that mean we all become "tree hugging" environmental activists and drive electric cars? No, but our grandchildren may wish we had.

Enjoying life responsibly means that we stop being greedy, wasteful and blind. It means we respect science and resist greedy and power hungry politicians who tell it's all about money and the economy. It's not.

Voices both Ancient and Modern

An awareness of universal consciousness is the basis for the ethical systems taught by Buddha and Jesus. Buddha is very clear in his belief that our sense of "self" is only an illusion (maya). He saw everything as various manifestations of just one thing. While he could not express it fully in words, he expressed it through a life of simplicity and compassion, supported by regular periods of meditation.

Buddha had an obvious influence on Jesus – if not through Buddhist missionaries, then directly through the universal field of awareness they both experienced so fully. 500 years before Jesus said "do unto others as you would have them do unto you", Buddha said "Do not do unto others what you would not have them do unto you". Jesus took Buddha's statement to a higher level, just like he did the Law of Moses when he transcended all the "thou shall nots" with a command to simply love your neighbor as yourself.

My point is: the love and compassion that Jesus and Buddha taught came from their realization that all human beings are ultimately the manifestation of one thing.

It may seem odd that while one of my goals in writing this book is to free my readers from religion, I keep referring to Jesus and Buddha. The reason is I see Jesus and Buddha, not as religious figures, but as two of many historical figures who saw a bigger picture than most. In spite of how long ago they lived, I happen to believe people like Jesus and Buddha still have much to teach us.

I also mention Jesus often, hoping to help Christians see Jesus differently than how the church presents him.

There are many Christians in the United States who seem to care about Jesus. How much healthier our society would be if they would open themselves up to a healthier and more accurate version of Jesus. How refreshing it would be if Christians would focus on the teachings of Jesus rather than viewing him as little more than a free ticket to heaven.

According to the Bible, on the night before he died, Jesus prayed that we would all experience the same oneness he experienced with "abba"

– an Aramaic word that expresses the intimate relationship between parent and child.

He repeatedly stated that we must die to self in order to experience the larger self which he also called the "kingdom of heaven" or the "kingdom of God". There are other verses in the Christian Bible that point to this idea of oneness – our being part of one "body", our being "branches" on one "vine", our being "in Christ". Based on such ideas, it is not a stretch at all to see Jesus as a Mediterranean Buddha crucified for his radical and threatening new dharma.

It was his awareness of the oneness we all share that naturally led to his radical ideas about not judging, turning the other cheek, unlimited forgiveness, unconditional love, loving your enemies, showing mercy to all, healing the sick, setting the captives free, feeding the hungry, clothing the naked, selling your possessions and giving the money to the poor, non-violence, inclusiveness, loving your neighbor as yourself and not fearing death.

According to Jesus, knowing who we really are sets us free to laugh, love, share and forgive in a radical way.

For most Christians, the mission of Jesus was to save people from sin. And sin is usually understood as the breaking of commandments by individuals. An objective reading of the life of Jesus, as recorded in the Bible, however, clearly shows that the primary mission of Jesus was to save people from pain and suffering, not sin.

Jesus is depicted as a healer and a teacher more than anything else. And his teachings have far more to do with helping the sick and the poor than condemning sinners.

When you look at people and the society around you, do you start by looking at the pain or the sin? And when you look at sin, do you look at individual sin or structural sin? Jesus always started with people's pain. When he occasionally did talk about sin, it was usually structural sin - the greedy and corrupt political and religious systems that keep people poor, powerless and exploited.

Some will justify their neglect of the poor by reminding us that Jesus said "the poor are with you always." If he did say that, it was because he knew there would always be economic systems that exploit the poor. He certainly was not suggesting that his followers neglect the poor.

Many Christians are against the government helping the poor. These extreme libertarians argue that Jesus only mentioned individuals helping the poor voluntarily, and he never talked about government assistance. Jesus never mentioned homosexuality either, but that doesn't stop many of these same people from condemning the LBGT community. We believe what we want to believe and always find ways to justify our beliefs.

If the majority of Americans decide voluntarily that they want taxes to pay for everyone's education, healthcare, social security and other social safety nets, so be it. So called "followers of Jesus" who argue that Jesus would oppose that, do not know Jesus. The key to being happy, at least according to great life coaches like Jesus and Buddha, is learning to be generous and kind to others, both as individuals and as a society.

Let's jump forward 2000 years. One of the fundamental truths of modern science is that all things are really just one thing. The fabric of reality is continuous and there is no clear distinction between where one thing ends and another thing begins.

"Non-locality" is just one of several insights from quantum physics that demonstrates this. Entangled atoms have a mysterious "oneness" with each other, even when they are light years apart in space. Changing one will instantaneously affect the other regardless of distance. Something seems to be connecting everything at a deep, fundamental level.

Many of us grew up viewing the atom somewhat like we view the solar system - a nucleus of protons and neutrons in the center with several electrons orbiting. Actually, electrons are more like the wave of potentiality we described earlier. Their exact position cannot be determined in the way we normally think. They probably exist in a particular place near the nucleus but can potentially exist anywhere in the universe.

In other words, the atoms that comprise your body are concentrated in your body, but also merge with the atoms in my body as well as those in distant stars. We are not the separate beings we think we are. Again, one cannot escape the ethical implications of such oneness. Enjoy life fully, but don't ignore the broader dimensions of what you are.

If there is one universal consciousness at the heart of everything, and if our conscious awareness flows from that one universal awareness; ultimate reality is both singular and plural. We see the plurality in our individuality, diversity, war, sickness, pain, death, gender, jealousy, fear, and the yen and yang of existence.

But beyond the plurality there is a deeper singularity – a oneness. Not neglecting the singularity leads to peace, mercy, grace, forgiveness, patience, unity, trust, hope, wholeness and love. Understanding and focusing on the singularity sets us free and allows us to enjoy life responsibly.

Pain and Suffering

"If happy I can be I will, if suffer I must I can,"
William Faulkner

"A student, filled with emotion and crying, implored, "Why is there so much suffering?"
Suzuki Roshi replied, "No reason." Shunryu Suzuki

Allow me to share a few final words regarding pain and suffering. Why does life hurt so much? Much of the world's suffering seems to stem from ignorance and other types of human brokenness. The Bible admits as much when it has Jesus praying for those who were crucifying him, "Father, forgive them, **they know not what they do**."

The Biblical admonitions to forgive and not judge suggest that humans need educating and healing rather than condemnation and punishment. We do horrible things to ourselves, each other and our planet - mostly due to blindness and brokenness.

Of course, natural causes of suffering like earthquakes and hurricanes can't be blamed on ignorance or human brokenness. They have to be attributed to natural causes, or what insurance policies call "acts of God". Here's a summary of how religion has answered the question of human suffering over the centuries. It basically comes down to three approaches.

Free Will

A common approach is to blame the world's pain on some kind of "God given" free will. Even earthquakes and other natural disasters are God's judgment on the misuse of free will by our earliest ancestors. This approach only changes the question to why a loving God would give his creation such dangerous free will in the first place.

God is omniscient so he knows what will happen. A God who gives humans that kind of free will would be like a parent who gives a child a loaded gun or a hand grenade. Any such parent, God included, should be charged with child endangerment.

Beyond the obvious religious inconsistencies, the concept of free will is also being challenged by science. There is mounting evidence that human free will is limited at best, and most likely an illusion. Either way, the concept of free will does little to help us confront a world so saturated with pain. It only adds guilt to the pain.

Growing Pains

Another approach to explaining pain is that God or some other universal intelligence allows suffering as a necessary component in our evolution. The claim is that evolution will finally lead to something good and worthwhile – the suffering will be justified. In other words, the end will justify the means.

This explanation obviously requires some kind of future "heaven" for all conscious beings. The billions of humans, who must suffer now in order to attain a future utopia, must somehow share in that future utopia. Otherwise, those born during this era of suffering get a very raw deal.

The problem is that traditional religious ideas related to "heaven" seem like myth and fairy tale to a growing number of people. Perhaps reincarnation offers a more believable scenario, but, again, conclusive evidence is hard to come by.

Bottom line: there may or may not be a final state of existence that justifies our current suffering. Only time will tell. Either way, the pain still hurts tremendously and often feels unjustifiable.

Scary Dream

A third explanation for suffering has more of an Eastern flavor. We touched on it earlier. It suggests that we are all incarnations of some higher consciousness, and that universal consciousness is simply experiencing all the possibilities of physical existence - pleasure and pain - through our physical bodies.

In other words, our present suffering is somewhat like a video game or a scary dream. Our only hope is that, at death, we will finally stop playing or finally wake up. The pain is temporary and ultimately not real. For many, this approach may be logical, but it's still somewhat cold and perhaps minimizes the pain we experience. The agony of pain remains.

A Better Response

When you're suffering or sharing in the suffering of a loved one, does it help to view the suffering as a necessary growing pain or a bad dream? Millions gain comfort from these ideas. But for millions of others, these explanations simply do not justify the indescribable amount of pain and suffering in our world.

So that leads to a fourth approach that is more a response than an explanation. Perhaps the best response to suffering is not trying to explain it. Simply accept it and be grateful for the gift of life.

Personally, I'm inspired by people who accept suffering as part of life. They don't try to explain it. They do what they can to lessen it, but they have also come to terms with it. They are grateful for having lived, and they focus on the good. If there's something more later on, that will be icing on the cake. Either way, they've made peace with what is.

When confronted with the suffering of others, we should try to lessen their pain. Sometimes all we can do is be there, but never under-estimate the value of your presence. People often worry about what they're going to say to someone with cancer or someone who lost a loved one. Truthfully, you don't have to say anything - and perhaps should not say anything. Just be there. Beyond that, trust your instincts and don't under-estimate the value of simple acts of kindness.

When my mom and dad were dying, I tried to be there as much as possible. I also tried to make sure my parents were getting the best medical care available to them. I tried to pay attention to little things that doctors and nurses could not know about or respond to.

Sometimes, I reminisced and talked about happy things. Sometimes I played their favorite music. Mostly I just listened and sat there. Even when they were not fully conscious, I shared my fondest memories with them, held their hand and told them how much I loved them. I tried to be there.

What about the suffering and death of children? That has to be the hardest thing of all. How do you bear watching your own child suffer? You desperately want to do something to rescue them or take their place. But you can't. You pray, or you lose your faith and stop praying. You cry and get angry. But nothing helps. Again, sometimes all you can do is be there.

I can't imagine the pain of losing a child. I've been told you gradually get stronger and find a way to bear the pain, but nothing is ever the same. I hesitate to even write about it.

If you have lost a child, I pray there comes a time when you can remember your loved one and smile - when you can be grateful for the time you had with them. I pray you feel their presence from time to time and find hope.

"No man is an island." We share the world's pain. When at our best, we feel the world's pain and do what we can to lessen it. As we find the freedom to enjoy life more fully, hopefully we will also find the freedom to see our larger self and enjoy life more responsibly and more generously.

Sister Moon

Like you,
Without an ego,
Only reflecting the light of the sun;
My desire is
That I, too,
Can shed my ego,
And only reflect the light
That shines within all living things.

As you spend most of your time
Being less than full,
Letting the stars light up the dark sky;
My desire is
That I, too,
Can spend most of my time
Being less than full of myself,
Letting the light of everything around me
Reveal my larger self.

As you wax and wane
Month after month,
My desire is
That I, too,
Can accept the waxing and waning of life,
Grateful for what has been and what will be,
Accepting what is.

Epilogue

5 Stages of Freedom

Psychologists and grief counselors often talk about "5 stages of grief". We all go through these stages in some form or fashion when faced with our own impending death or the death of a loved one.

We also experience them in a more general way when new truths force us to let go of long held beliefs that are fundamental to our world view and our sense of self.

As we grow older, ideas that were once familiar and comfortable no longer ring true. Life forces us to accept new ideas that are less familiar and less comfortable. What follows is a painful adjustment, a "dark night of the soul" that mirrors the classical stages of grief described below.

The good news is that on the other side of this process we discover freedom and joy. What many call the "5 Stages of Grief" can also be called the "5 Stages of Freedom".

Denial

The first stage is denial. We all start there. As a society, we tend to deny the reality of death and other uncomfortable truths in numerous ways. Religion is one of the main ways. It begins in childhood when we are told that grandma or grandpa went to heaven to be with Jesus.

For me personally, this stage of denial was reflected in my early commitment to traditional religious ideas involving conversions, resurrections, angels, scriptures, heavens and hells. I needed certainty. I needed to be in control.

Not just religion, but various cultural norms and memes evolve to help us live in denial of uncomfortable truths. Rather than tell us the truth, politicians often exploit our fear of the truth in order to maintain power. All this makes it easy for individuals to follow the herd and keep avoiding the painful journey that leads to freedom.

But truth cannot be avoided forever. The next stage is inevitable.

Bargaining

As we journey through life, most of us will be confronted with uncomfortable truths we can no longer deny. So we begin to bargain.

When the religious framework I committed to as a young minister began to crumble, I still wasn't ready to acknowledge that the entire system was fatally flawed. I convinced myself that it could be repaired and remodeled.

I started exploring more liberal versions of Christianity, broader concepts of God, less literal approaches to the Bible, and more creative ways to do church. I desperately reasoned, "Surely, I can adjust old ideas to accommodate new truths, without turning my entire worldview upside down".

The same bargaining process takes place within each of us when deeply held views begin to unravel and force us out of our comfort zone. We try to minimize the damage and hold on to as much of the past as we can.

We may search for different ways to justify our positions or simply retreat to people who think like us. We always find ways to believe what we want to believe.

But truth is stubborn and unrelenting. Once the dam cracks, there's no stopping the flood that follows.

Anger

Some of what I discovered during the "bargaining" stage continues to hold value for me, but overall, my previous world view could not be salvaged. I became angry.

While I tried to express my anger responsibly, I became very critical of preachers, politicians, my own selfishness, wealthy elites and the blind masses that allow themselves to be exploited so easily.

The exploitation I have described in this book continues to make me angry at times. Obviously, the stages described here sometimes repeat and overlap.

As societies evolve, painful transitions that inevitably take place are always marked by anger. Unfortunately, anger all too often leads to violence. History clearly demonstrates how cruel and relentless religious and political forces can be when threatened by painful truth.

When individuals or groups become angry, you can bet their safe and familiar world is being threatened by facts they can no longer deny or negotiate. Anger is obviously more emotional than rational, and, like water, it will usually follow the path of least resistance.

Anger cannot be avoided, but hopefully we can recognize it for what it is and express it responsibly and non-violently.

Depression

As anger runs its course, there is often the temptation to give up, stop searching and become cynical. There may be a loss of hope and motivation, along with other obvious symptoms of depression. Many will turn to alcohol or some other short term pleasure to ease the pain.

I went through periods of cynicism and sadness when my long held worldviews finally collapsed. There seemed to be no explanation or solution for the human condition. No religious or philosophical system held an answer. Does anything really matter? This is the "dark night of the soul" that so many have written about across the centuries.

Not just individuals, but societies can also become depressed, stagnant and unhealthy. This is reflected in growing crime rates, poor health outcomes, distrust of institutions, wide spread fear mongering, elevated drug use, high suicide rates and a general reduction in overall quality of life.

Acceptance

Fortunately, depression and anger do not have to have the final word. I have gradually made peace with what is. I'm learning to let go of what no longer works and embrace new truth, regardless of where it comes from. I'm learning to accept the roller coaster that life is and be grateful for getting to take the ride.

I continue to be intrigued with the idea of one universal consciousness. While I cannot name it or explain it, I enjoy exploring the possibilities it raises regarding life and death. Personally, I'm freer than I have ever been, and I am trying to enjoy life responsibly.

We can all accept new truth, adjust accordingly and begin to enjoy life more fully than ever before. We can experience freedom from religious and political exploitation, as well as the negative forces of addiction and fear.

We can make peace with death and focus on life. We can learn to live in the present moment with optimism, joy and integrity. We can be thankful for what we have now and keep exploring new possibilities for the future. We can learn to both embrace and trust the Mystery of existence.

As a society, we can acknowledge past failures and affirm that national well-being requires going forward, not backward. We can acknowledge our oneness and affirm that we all do better when we all do better. We can keep evolving toward that ideal society envisioned by prophets, philosophers, fairytales and dreamers.

Maybe we will. Maybe not. I wonder.

In the meantime, I leave you with this blessing.

May you remain free
From exploitation, addiction and fear.
May you discover a larger self
And enjoy life responsibly.

Questions or comments: johnalanshope@gmail.com

John Alan Shope

Appendix

Inconsistencies in Biblical accounts of Jesus' death:

Mark, Matthew and Luke say Jesus was arrested the day after Passover.
John says Jesus was arrested on the day before Passover.

Mark, Matthew and Luke say Jesus was silent before Pilate except for saying, "You have said so."
John says Jesus talked with Pilate at length.

Mark, Matthew and Luke say Simon carried Jesus' cross.
John says Jesus carried his own cross.

Mark, Matthew and Luke say the crucifixion began at 9am.
John says the crucifixion began at noon.

Mark and Matthew say both men crucified with Jesus hurled insults at him.
Luke says one of the men hurled insults while the other defended Jesus. Jesus said to that man, "Today you will be with me in paradise."

Mark, Matthew and Luke say Mary, Mary Magdalene and other women watched from a distance.
John says Mary, Mary Magdalene and John were near the cross, and Jesus asked John to care for his mother.

Mark and Matthew say Jesus' final words were, "My God, my God, why have you forsaken me?"
Luke says Jesus' final words were, "Father, into your hands I commit my spirit."
John says Jesus' final words were, "It is finished."

Mark, Matthew, Luke and John say Joseph of Arimathea buried Jesus.
Acts says Jewish rulers, who did not know Jesus, buried him.

Inconsistencies in Biblical accounts of Jesus' resurrection:

Matthew says Mary Magdalene and another Mary first saw the empty tomb.
Mark says Mary Magdalene, Mary the mother of James and Salome first saw the empty tomb.
Luke says Mary Magdalene, Mary the mother of James, Joanna and at least two other women first saw the empty tomb.
John says Mary Magdalene went to the tomb alone, saw the stone removed, ran to find Peter, and returned to the tomb with Peter and another disciple.

Matthew says the women saw an angel sitting on the stone that had been rolled away. Roman guards were also present.
Mark says the women saw a young man in a white robe sitting inside the tomb.
Luke says the women saw two men in dazzling apparel at the tomb.
John says Mary and Peter and another disciple initially find just an empty tomb. Peter and the other disciple enter the tomb, find it empty, then leave. Mary Magdalene then sees two angels in white.

Paul (1 Cor. 15) says Jesus appeared first to Peter, then the 12 disciples – no mention of the women.
Luke says Jesus appears first to two unknown disciples, then to Peter, then to all eleven disciples – no mention of women.
Mark and John say Jesus appears first to Mary Magdalene then later to the eleven disciples.
Matthew says Jesus appears first to Mary Magdalene and another Mary, and finally to the eleven disciples.

Matthew says Mary Magdalene and the other Mary recognized Jesus.
John says Mary Magdalene didn't recognize Jesus.

Matthew says Jesus let Mary Magdalene and another Mary hold his feet.
John says Jesus would not let Mary Magdalene touch him.

Matthew and Mark say the disciples met Jesus in Galilee.
Luke and Acts say the disciples met Jesus in Jerusalem.

Mark and Luke say Jesus ascended on or near the same day as the resurrection.
Acts says Jesus ascended at least 40 days after his resurrection.
Matthew and John do not mention Jesus' ascension.

Evolution of Jesus becoming Son of God in Bible

Most Biblical scholars are convinced that Jesus never claimed to be the Jewish messiah or the Son of God. According to the Bible, his favorite expression for himself was "Son of Man". In fact, to help explain why Jesus never claimed to be the Jewish Messiah or the Son of God, Mark (the earliest gospel) has Jesus telling his disciples on several occasions not to tell anyone who he is.

So how did Jesus later evolve from "Son of Man" to "Son of God"? In the ancient world, it was common for exceptional people to be taken up to heaven at death and be adopted as "Sons of God". According to legend, this happened to Romulus, the founder of Rome. According to Jewish legend, it also happened to Moses. After Jesus' death, the earliest followers of Jesus started believing that he too had been taken up to heaven at death and adopted as God's son.

This view is reflected in Acts 13:33 where an early sermon by Peter states that at Jesus' resurrection, God made Jesus his son and fulfilled what was written in Psalm 2, "You are my son; today I have become your father."

The idea of Jesus' divine sonship kept evolving. Interestingly, by the time the gospel of Mark was written, many were teaching that Jesus became God's son at his baptism rather than at his resurrection. In Mark 1:10 we read, "Just as Jesus was coming up out of the water, he saw heaven being torn open and the Spirit descending on him like a dove. And a voice came from heaven: 'You are my Son, whom I love; with you I am well pleased.'"

By the time the gospels of Matthew and Luke were written (15 to 20 years later), many were teaching that Jesus became God's son at birth. Unlike Mark, both Matthew and Luke contain the story of Jesus' virgin birth. In Luke 1, an angel tells Mary, "The Holy Spirit will come upon you, and the power of the Most High will overshadow you. So the holy one to be born will be called the Son of God."

Finally, by the time the gospel of John was written (15 to 20 years after Matthew and Luke), many followers of Jesus were teaching that Jesus had always been God's son. John does not mention the virgin birth, but rather begins, "In the beginning was the Word, and the Word was with God, and the Word was God. He was with God in the beginning," (John 1:1-2). In other words, Jesus had always existed as the Son of God.

Over the next 200 years the debate centered around what it meant for Jesus to be the Son of God. Ultimately, the doctrine of the Trinity became the official explanation at the Council of Nicaea in 325 AD.

Parallels between the lives of Buddha and Jesus as presented in both Buddhist and Christian writings.

Both born as an incarnate god.
Both born from a virgin mother.
Birth claimed as a divine event and prophesied as the same.
Birth attended by singing angels.
Birth attended by wise men bearing gifts.
As a child astounded teachers with knowledge.
Fasted in the wilderness for forty days.
Tempted while alone by the devil.
After the devil left, supernatural events occurred.
Were vegetarians (fish excepted).
Began ministry at thirty years of age.
Attracted large following mostly from lower classes.
Attracted disciples who traveled with him.
Attracted one disciple who was treacherous.
Changed disciples' names.
Encouraged celibacy for their disciples.
Consecrated or baptized in a holy river.
Itinerant ministry instead of at a fixed place.
Performed miracles such as curing blindness.
Renounced worldly riches and required the same of their disciples.
Ministered to outcasts.
Advocated universal love and peace.
Taught mostly through use of parables.
Triumphal entries (in Jerusalem and Rajagripa).
Gave major sermon from a mound.
Disregarded by the dominant religious elite (Pharisees and Brahmans).
Just before death dispatched disciples to preach in other areas.
Death accompanied by a supernatural event.

Parallels between statements attributed to Buddha and Jesus as presented in Buddhist and Christian scriptures.

BUDDHA: "Perishable is a city built on sand."
JESUS: "A foolish man, which built his house on sand."

BUDDHA: "Confess before the world the sins you have committed."
JESUS: "Therefore confess your sins one to another, and pray one for another, that you may be healed."

BUDDHA: "Let all sins that were committed in this world fall on me, that the world may be delivered."
THE GOSPEL OF JOHN REGARDING JESUS: "Behold the Lamb of God, who takes away the sins of the world."

BUDDHA: "Consider others as yourself."
JESUS: "Do to others as you would have them do to you."

BUDDHA: "If anyone should give you a blow with his hand, with a stick, or with a knife, you should abandon all desires and utter no evil words."
JESUS: "If anyone strikes you on the cheek, offer the other also."

BUDDHA: "Hatreds do not cease in this world by hating, but by love: this is an eternal truth. Overcome anger by love, overcome evil by good."
JESUS: "Love your enemies, do good to those who hate, bless those who curse you, pray for those who abuse you."

BUDDHA: "Let your thoughts of boundless love pervade the whole world."
JESUS: "This is my commandment, that you love one another as I have loved you."

BUDDHA: "Do not look at the faults of others or what others have done or not done; observe what you yourself have done and have not done."
JESUS: "Let anyone among you who is without sin be the first to cast a stone at her."

BUDDHA: "The light of the sun and the moon illuminates the whole world, both him who does well and him who does ill, both him who stands high and him who stands low."

JESUS: "Your father in heaven makes his sun rise on the evil and on the good, and sends rain on the righteous and on the unrighteous."

BUDDHA: "The avaricious do not go to heaven, the foolish do not extol charity. The wise one, however, rejoicing in charity, becomes thereby happy in the beyond."

JESUS: "If you wish to be perfect, go sell your possessions, and give the money to the poor, and you will have treasure in heaven."

A Most Memorable Sunday Morning

There were a little over 100 in attendance that chilly, fall Sunday morning. I had been the Pastor for almost 5 years. As most Baptist preachers do, especially in the Bible Belt, I stepped up to the pulpit, Bible in hand, and started my sermon.

But it was not what anyone expected. "This morning I want to talk about authority. When it comes down to what you believe about life, death, God, the world, who or what do you ultimately trust? Most of you, as good Baptists, will say "the Bible". I used to say that, too. But no longer.

Please hear me out. As your Bible commands you, be patient, kind and merciful. Listen till the end and I will do something very unusual and unexpected.

I proclaim to you this morning that the Spirit of Christ within you, not the Bible, is your ultimate authority. It always has been and always will be. It was for Jesus.

You say: "But then everyone will simply believe what they want. There will be no consistency." Yes, but it's that way already.

When you read a verse in the Bible that you can't accept at face value, because it contradicts another verse that our spirit overwhelmingly assures us to be true; you say, "Well, I can't explain that. I don't know."

I'll say of that same problematic verse, "That's simply not true. The Bible is wrong there." My statement is more shocking, but the end result is the same. We ignore the disturbing verse and follow the verse we both know to be true.

Jesus did this, and it ultimately led to his crucifixion. According to Matthew, he said, "You have heard it said, 'An eye for an eye and a tooth for a tooth.'" (He was quoting the Bible.)

He continued, to the amazement of all, "But I say to you, love your enemies and forgive those who persecute you."

Jesus allowed the Spirit of God within him to challenge and ultimately override the Bible. He constantly referred to the Spirit, and finally told his disciples, "The Spirit (not the scripture) will guide you to all truth."

Do you know the history of the Bible? Most of the Bible (the Old Testament) was written long before Jesus was born. The rest of the Bible (the New Testament) was written 25 to 70 years after Jesus died. Over half the New Testament was written by people who never met Jesus or heard him speak.

Paul, who wrote half the New Testament, and who many claim to be the architect of Christianity, only experienced the spirit of Jesus many years after Jesus died. Luke got his information about Jesus from interviewing other people. Mark got his information about Jesus mostly from Peter. We're not sure who wrote several books, including the book of Hebrews.

I'm simply reminding you that Jesus never wrote anything, and neither did most of those who actually knew and heard him first hand. Furthermore, much of what was written about Jesus after he died is not in the Bible.

Almost 300 years after Jesus died, the emerging Roman Catholic Church saw the need for more consistency regarding what Christians believed. At the time, there were numerous versions of Christianity and numerous versions of Jesus. So in 325 AD the emperor of Rome called all the leading Bishops of the church to Rome to decide once and for all which early writings should be considered true, and which early writings should be considered untrue.

As you might expect, there were personalities and politics involved, and the final decision was not unanimous. But a final decision was reached, and thus we have the Bible. Still, the Bible was the product of a very fallible human institution; which later claimed that only the top leaders of the institution could interpret the Bible correctly.

Interestingly, when Martin Luther instigated the Protestant Reformation over 1000 years later, challenging the authority of this institution, which

had come to be known as the Roman Catholic Church, he did so by primarily trusting the Spirit within him, not just the Bible.
In fact he felt that the book of James and the book of Revelation should not be in the Bible, because they contradicted what the Spirit was revealing to him about grace.

Don't misunderstand me. I love the Bible, and I will continue to preach from the Bible. The truth it contains can make the world a better place. But only if we approach it honestly, and if we are not afraid to admit when it's wrong. as did Jesus, and many others, both then and now.

Bottom line, as Jesus both taught and exemplified, when the Bible says you should kill your enemies, it's wrong. When the Bible implies that gay people are condemned to hell, it's wrong. When the Bible says women should always submit to their husbands and be silent in the church, it's wrong. When the Bible is interpreted to say (it never actually uses these words) that anyone who does not accept Jesus as their personal Lord and Savior is condemned to an eternal hell, it's wrong. When the Bible is interpreted to say that Christianity is the only true religion, it's wrong.

There are many things in the Bible that are absolutely true, and we ignore them at our own peril. But only the Spirit within you can recognize these truths. And your failure to let the Spirit within you recognize and give you the courage to admit the many things in the Bible that are not true, will only leave you confused and out of step with the Jesus you claim to follow.

There will be many times when you will have to choose between believing something in the Bible and believing something revealed to you by the Spirit of Christ within you.

So, here's my promised surprise ending. In closing, I want you all to close your eyes, and just be still before God.

If you cannot accept what I have said this morning; if you must continue to believe every word in the Bible, regardless of how disturbing and inconsistent it is; if you cannot at least be open to my words, I invite you to lovingly and respectfully stand up and leave. I will not take it personally. I will respect your decision. I know that for many of you I am challenging one of your most deeply held beliefs, and I understand the fear and pain involved In letting such beliefs go. Believe me, I have been there. But now I'm here, and I understand if you can no longer walk along side me.

On the other hand, if the Spirit within you is telling you that I may be right; if you are open to continuing with me this more open journey toward truth; if you are willing to challenge human traditions, human institutions and human books; then I invite you to remain seated as others leave.

I believe in Democracy. So if, when we all open our eyes, less than 63 people remain, I will resign as of today. If 63 or more are still here, I will continue as your Pastor; and we will continue this challenging journey toward truth together. We will face the risks together, knowing there will be failures and successes; but trusting the Spirit of Christ, who lives within all people, to ultimately guide us, and all of humanity, to the truth.

I hear many people leaving, as they must. Make your decision as we wait a just few more minutes.

Now let's all open our eyes and see what this group of people has decided. Ok. It's what I expected...

John Alan Shope

Additional Resources

Websites:

Westar Institute	https://www.westarinstitute.org/

Institute of Noetic Sciences http://noetic.org/research/research-lab

Freedom from Religion Foundation	https://ffrf.org/

Yeshua (Jesus) Before 30AD	http://30ce.com/

Horizon Research Foundation http://www.horizonresearch.org/

Forever Family Foundation
https://forever-family-foundation.herokuapp.com/

Spiritual Understanding
http://selfguided.spiritualunderstanding.org/

Religion For Breakfast http://religionforbreakfast.com/

The Monroe Institute https://www.monroeinstitute.org/

Mark Hyman, MD	http://drhyman.com/

Cleveland Clinic	https://my.clevelandclinic.org/health

Richard Rohr, Center for Action and Contemplation
https://cac.org/

Books

A Brief History of Christianity, Carter Lindberg 2006

The Tao of Psychology, Jean Shinoda Bolen, MD 1982

The Gospel of Jesus, Robert Funk and Author Dewey

Quantum Physics of Consciousness, Lana Tao 2011

Eternal Life, A new Vision, John Shelby Spong 2009

The Tao of Physics, Fritjof Capra 1991

Origins of Consciousness, Adrian David Nelson 2015

The Original Jesus, Elmer Gruber & Holger Kersten 1995

The Physics of Consciousness, Evan Harris Walker 2000

Honest to Jesus, Robert W Funk 1996

The Christian Agnostic, Leslie Weatherhead 1978

How Much Is Enough? Arthur Simon 2006

Beyond Belief, Elaine Pagels 2005

Infinite In All Directions, Freeman Dyson 1989

The large, the Small and the Human Mind, Roger Penrose

Flatland, Edwin A. Abbott 1992

Meeting Jesus Again For the First Time, Marcus Borg 1995

A History of God, Karen Armstrong 1994

Happy Are You Poor, Thomas Dubay 2003

The Meditative Mind, Daniel Goleman 1977

It Just Is, John Alan Shope 2016

Jesus, Buddha and Science, John Alan Shope 2016

Be Free

John Alan Shope

Made in the USA
Columbia, SC
25 June 2018